they SNOOZE you LOSE

Lynell Burmark

they SNOOZE *you* LOSE

The Educator's Guide to Successful Presentations

JB JOSSEY-BASS

Published by Jossey-Bass
A Wiley Imprint
989 Market Street, San Francisco, CA 94103-1741—www.josseybass.com

Image credits appear on page 259

Readers should be aware that Internet websites offered as citations and/or sources for further information may have changed or disappeared between the time this was written and when it is read.

Limit of Liability/Disclaimer of Warranty: While the publisher and author have used their best efforts in preparing this book, they make no representations or warranties with respect to the accuracy or completeness of the contents of this book and specifically disclaim any implied warranties of merchantability or fitness for a particular purpose. No warranty may be created or extended by sales representatives or written sales materials. The advice and strategies contained herein may not be suitable for your situation. You should consult with a professional where appropriate. Neither the publisher nor author shall be liable for any loss of profit or any other commercial damages, including but not limited to special, incidental, consequential, or other damages.

Jossey-Bass books and products are available through most bookstores. To contact Jossey-Bass directly call our Customer Care Department within the U.S. at 800-956-7739, outside the U.S. at 317-572-3986, or fax 317-572-4002.

Jossey-Bass also publishes its books in a variety of electronic formats. Some content that appears in print may not be available in electronic books.

Library of Congress Cataloging-in-Publication Data
Burmark, Lynell, (date)–
  They snooze, you lose : the educator's guide to successful presentations/ Lynell Burmark.
    p. cm.
  Includes index.
  ISBN 978-0-470-90290-5 (pbk.)
  1. Educational innovations. 2. Classroom environment. 3. Computer-assisted instruction. 4. Teaching. 5. Learning. I. Title.
  LB1027.B825 2011
  371.3—dc22
                    2010053640

Printed in the United States of America

FIRST EDITION

PB Printing   10 9 8 7 6 5 4 3 2 1

Contents

About the DVD   *vii*

Foreword   *xi*

Acknowledgments   *xiii*

Introduction   *xv*

About the author   *xvii*

Part 1 Evolution

1 Tweaking presentations **3**

Templates, color, and type

2 Creating slides and handouts **25**

Powerful role for slides; complementary job for handouts

3 Celebrating presenters **43**

Lecturer + entertainer + motivator = educator

Part 2 Revolution

4 Ringing CHIMES[2] **61**

Connections, humor, images, music, emotion, story, and senses

5 Making connections **69**

Creating context; ten-minute limit, 10:2 presentations; Wordles

6 Harnessing humor **93**

Wit, mirth, and laughter; the humor zone; resources

7 Starting with images **109**

    Setting the stage, reducing text, color power, pictorial effect

8 Playing music **141**

    Dictating appropriate emotional states; music and learning; your Beatles

9 Tapping emotion **157**

    Sticky like Post-it notes; statistics versus emotional appeal; HeartMath

10 Telling stories **175**

    Stories organize our worlds; progressive story; writing the future

11 Engaging senses **195**

    Multisensory learning, anchor images, dual channels, popcorn to remember

Part 3 Resolution

12 Putting it all together **215**

    Review of ten starter strategies for avoiding presentation pitfalls

    Notes   *229*

    Index   *249*

    Credits   *259*

    How to use the DVD   *261*

About the DVD

Read me

Gives you an outline of the content on the DVD, including Mac and Windows players for the HyperStudio slideshows ("stacks") on the disc.

Book support

Chapter-by-chapter supplemental color images and slideshows to go along with the book. (This will be particularly helpful to those of you using this book to teach a course. Think of it as your preparation handed to you on a disc!)

Don't miss Dave's résumé and the LCD shootout plus the "yellow" PowerPoint showing how to reference citations. (And that's just part of Chapter One.)

Bonus images and slideshows

Hundreds of high-quality, royalty-free images and slideshows for teachers, students, and presenters to apply and extend ideas and activities from the book. (We understand that finding and sizing images can be time consuming. Think of this section as your starter image library.)

Contributed for educational use only, there are hundreds of breathtakingly beautiful images of places from the incomparable Sedona, Arizona, to Ylvingen, Norway (home of a wildly popular Norwegian soap opera). Don't miss the Story starters.ppt—great for creative writing, drama classes, or sponge activities in a variety of classroom settings.

Royalty-free music

Original compositions (instrumentals) in a variety of genres as well as songs performed by Rosko the Band (Liverpool, England) and yours truly singing "Don't Blame the Sunshine."

Make sure to check out "Grand Entrance" and "Moody Melodies," which are medleys of short clips to dramatize the impact of music in presentations and for affecting emotional states.

Dedication

*To five generations of family who have loved me
unconditionally:*

*from Grandma Burmark, who read me stories,
to my great-niece Taylor, who has me read stories to her,*

 *and especially to my brother,
Wes, who patiently and insightfully
read and commented on this story,
now offered lovingly from our family
to yours.*

Foreword

Like a magician revealing her secrets to you, Dr. Burmark is incredibly generous with her advice and exquisitely entertaining as she delivers it. You will find yourself laughing at her insights and nodding at her understanding of the challenges and joys that educators face on a daily basis.

In the many years I've worked with Dr. Burmark and have seen her present, she has deployed technology with the best of us. She has consistently shared that, as much as tech tools can enhance the presenter's story, it's the story itself that is the key to the presentation's success. As your storyteller, Dr. Burmark brings tremendous experience to this book. An award-winning educator, she has taught at all levels from kindergarten through graduate school. She has given countless presentations to audiences of all sizes and has extensive experience with every idea shared in this book. If you are an educator, this is a Monday-morning book whose impact will be apparent the next time you or your students are preparing a presentation for anyone, from the classroom to the school board.

In the tradition of her classic book, *Visual Literacy: Learn to See, See to Learn,* and her popular live performances, Dr. Burmark stresses the visual aspect of presentations. ("First the image, then the words." "Words can only recall images we have already seen.") In this new book, she celebrates not only the visuals but also the synergy of adding music and humor and telling stories to make an emotional connection with the audience. She gives examples, resources, and replicable activities, and always practices what she preaches. Never more than ten minutes (or two pages) of lecture (text) without an activity to involve the audience (reader). The pacing of research-information-anecdotes and activities also makes this tome an ideal, ready-made textbook in which teachers and professors can "assign" the activities as in-class projects or homework for the course. The complementary DVD offers additional materials to make teaching this "course" a breeze!

Whether you use the book as a textbook or as an individual personal guide, every tip you try—and by the way they are all free—will make you a better presenter and ensure that you and your audience will have more fun in the process. Like Dr. Burmark, you can become a model presenter, one who tells your story with grace and humor, reaches hearts and minds, and transforms as well as informs those you touch with your magic and your truth.

DAVID THORNBURG
Recife, Brazil
Lake Barrington, Illinois
Adjunct professor, Walden University
Founder and director of global operations for the
Thornburg Center for Professional Development
www.tcpd.org
dthornburg@aol.com

Acknowledgments

As Nigerian proverb *"Ora na azu nwa"* and Hillary Clinton's *New York Times* best seller attest: "It takes a village to raise a child." It has taken a global village to "raise" this book and DVD.

From the dozens of respected researchers whose work I mined, Doc Childre and Martin Howard (*HeartMath*), Chip and Dan Heath (*Made to Stick*), Richard E. Mayer (*Multimedia Learning*), and John Medina (*Brain Rules*) stand out as absolute essentials.

Then there are the presentation gurus who have inspired my journey, starting with the wise and witty Tad Simons (former editor in chief of *Presentations Magazine*) and starring must-have authors like Nancy Duarte (*slide:ology, resonate*) and Garr Reynolds (*Presentation Zen* and *Presentation Zen Design*).

In categories by themselves are the inimitable Roger Wagner, creator of HyperStudio, who has offered his insightful thinking (which he calls a "stream of semi-consciousness") throughout the project, and my treasured mentor and friend Dick Bolles (*What Color Is Your Parachute?*), who helped me find my calling as a "stand-up comic, singing priest" and who freely gave permission to use his copyrighted materials in this book (see Chapters Four and Ten).

Photographers from Norway to Hawaii, Germany to Yosemite, the Grand Canyon to Brazil have generously donated their best work. (Please see the illustration credits at the end of the book and the specific photographers listed on the DVD.) I also deeply appreciate the good-humored folks (including many family members) who have posed for pictures to help make critical points in the book. Pictures of nieces Shanta Parasuraman and Stacie and Taylor Jensen are some of the most beautiful images in the book! And, as my brother Wes noted while photographing nieces Karly and Blair, "We're really lucky that the Burmark cousins had such good-looking kids!" Regarding the images, I also need to make special mention of the healing touch (and touch-ups) by Photoshop guru Lance Cadena, who transformed dozens of images not ready for prime time into the spectacular illustrations you are holding in your hands.

Colleagues and associates have not hesitated to advise—from Eric Dahm of 100% Educational Videos to Heather Johnston from Epson to all the pragmatic visionaries in the Thornburg Center and long-time friend (and constant source of joy and inspiration) Google Lit Trips founder Jerome Burg.

Special thanks must also go to the storytellers—Sara Armstrong, Jim Brazell, Hall Davidson, Steve Harrington, Rushton Hurley, AnnRené Joseph, Jason Ohler, Bernajean Porter, Gary Stager and David Thornburg—for connecting our hearts to theirs. And how can we ever thank the musicians for their inspiration (Dave Carroll) and their compositions and performances on the DVD (Tor Caspersen-Burmark and the always uplifting Lou Marzeles)?

As for publisher Jossey-Bass/Wiley, I'm especially indebted to Justin Frahm, who managed production, and senior editor Kate Bradford, who invited me to write this book and who—along with Wes Burmark, Tacoma Public Schools director of instructional technology—made sure that from the one hundred thousand words I wrote the very best fifty thousand were saved for you, the readers.

On a local level, there have been the neighbors who understood that "the book" had to come first and stood by me anyway: Rodger Bauer, Judy Beggs, Nada Boban, Marian Christensen, Herb Joly, Tom Mangano, Shirley Meloy—some brought me food, others remembered me in their prayers. And last but not least, there's my chiropractor and friend Dr. Rob Murray who keep my mouse-clicking muscles limber and who even contributed pictures from his African safari for the DVD!

For all these local and global friends and mentors, my heartfelt thanks and my profound wish that this book will honor your support and contributions, amplify your heart and your voice, and project your vision as well as mine.

And to all of you reading, welcome to the village.

Introduction

It's that nightmare again—the one where you are trapped in a mind-numbingly boring slideshow presentation. A cloak of darkness covers the room, periodically pierced by the flashing light of a glitzy slide transition. Bullets, up to a dozen per slide, zoom in from all directions. You duck, but the bullets keep coming, along with text too small to read on templates you've seen somewhere before. Typefaces dissolve as letters collide, and a line of text turns gray, ceding the spotlight to the next relentless row of words. Somewhere, from the shadows, a voice drones on.

Struggling to stay awake, you wonder: "Could this possibly get any worse?" And then, as your chin drops to your chest, you respond: "Only if it was *me* holding the remote."[1]

Your awakening intuition contends: "There must be a better way." And indeed there is—right here in your hands. You have picked up this book for a reason. Yes, it will help you create and deliver the presentation you have to give next week. It will also empower you to change the presentation practice of other educators who learn from your example. And, for you teachers and students who are using *They Snooze, You Lose* as a textbook, it will give you the research and practice, examples and illustrations, replicable activities, individual and group projects, comprehension and mastery checks, references, and resources you need to transform somniferous bullet points into presentations that keep everyone—including the presenter—engaged, involved, and awake!

Ah, but do you have the time and money to pull this off right now? Regarding the time commitment, researchers have documented that it takes less than four hours to read this book, cover to cover. As for the activities, if you are a classroom teacher, think of them as dozens of free, interactive lesson plans that you can adapt to use with your students. If you are an administrator or otherwise occupied outside the classroom, think of the relevant activities as guided practice for the creation of your own presentations. And watch for links to animated clips!

Grab a colleague or family member and share some popcorn during those hilarious albeit brief video moments. Popcorn is cheap and the laughter is free.

Speaking of free, assuming you already have an LCD projector, everything recommended here (beyond the popcorn and a few other inexpensive props) is f-r-e-e. That includes the material on the complementary DVD, which is packed with slideshows, additional images, royalty-free music files, and other resources.

Throughout the book, within the constraints of the print medium, I have tried to practice the techniques I preach for innovative presentations. Images and humor (my unique brand) abound, and you never have to read for more than five minutes before I make you laugh, think, share, apply, dance, create, spray chocolate, drink coffee—whatever it takes to caffeinate your experience so you neither snooze, nor lose.

Warm regards,

LYNELL BURMARK
Sunnyvale, California
www.educatebetter.org
lynell@educatebetter.org

About the author

Winner of Stanford University's prestigious Walter J. Gores Excellence in Teaching Award, Dr. Lynell Burmark is passionate about education and the potential for learners in her presentations and yours.

Lynell's extensive classroom experience spans kindergarten through graduate school; her visually enhanced presentations range from small-group seminars to keynotes and videoconferences for thousands of educators across the globe.

Her classic work, *Visual Literacy: Learn to See, See to Learn*, won the book of the year award for publisher ASCD. In *They Snooze, You Lose*, Lynell takes visual literacy to the next level with new research and more humorous insights, replicable activities for teachers and trainers, and practical applications for everyone wanting to craft and deliver "caffeinated" presentations.

Visit the website for more information about Dr. Burmark's background, publications, presentation offerings, and free resources including downloadable articles, videos, and banks of images suitable for educational use.

www.educatebetter.org
lynell@educatebetter.org

they
SNOOZE
you
LOSE

PART 1
Evolution

In the spirit of full disclosure, I should let you know right up front my not-so-hidden agenda in this book is to persuade you and your students to transform your slide shows into bullet-free presentations.

Think Gandhi. You do not need bullets to make your point.

In this first part, my plan is just to help you tweak your existing presentations so you can make a not-so-good thing better until you are ready to make a better thing your very best.

1

Tweaking presentations

Long before 1989, when PowerPoint was invented, I already felt the urge to make presentations. At age three, I recall standing on the platform of my hometown church singing "This Little Light of Mine" to a thousand-member congregation. The lyrics were easy to memorize:

> This little light of mine
> I'm gonna make it shine
> This little light of mine
> I'm gonna make it shine, shine, shine.

The melody was also pretty simple. Besides, I had been singing nonstop since the moment of conception (at least that was my mother's contention). I was all dolled up in my favorite pink nylon dress, feeling totally passionate about my message, and determined to convince every person present to get with the light-shining program. So, of course, while performing, I *had* to gesture with a lit candle. My mother tried to tell me that an unlit candle would do just as well, but there was no dissuading me. I don't think anyone present will ever forget that performance—especially my mother, who expected me to go up in flames every time I waved the candle anywhere near that pink nylon dress.

Activity 1.1

Recall a memorable presentation or performance that you have given (or attended). Write down the experience, including details that could help colleagues or classmates "see" what made it successful. Share those experiences, either in small groups or with the whole class. Comment on what you found striking in other people's presentations.

How many of those memorable performances involved Power-Point or some other presentation software? How has the world of presentations changed since 1989? What is it about PowerPoint that reduces passionate, articulate, charismatic experts in their fields to dull, rote, boring presenters? How do their colorful stories, exciting experiences, and brilliant insights fade into lifeless text on a drab and vapid background? Who convinced us that bullets could make our points more convincingly than we could?

Honestly, I can't tell you how in just over twenty years we have let it go this far. A few voices in the wilderness have tried to warn us: Edward Tufte,[1] Garr Reynolds,[2] Nancy Duarte,[3] for example. And some, including Roger Wagner,[4] Chip and Dan Heath,[5] and Daniel Pink,[6] have even dared to suggest that there might be a different path entirely. (See the Notes for brief descriptions of their work.) But the tide was too strong. Tad Simons, former editor in chief of *Presentations Magazine*, has estimated that some thirty million PowerPoints are given around the world every day.[7] With an average of thirty-three captive audience members for each presentation, that calculates to how many people blitzed by bullets? About a billion. Daily.

Please understand that I am not against computer-based slide-shows, just against letting them snuff out my creativity or constrain my capacity as a presenter. When a Wizard pops up to inform me how I want to lay out a particular slide, I click on the Close button and respectfully remind the little droid that *I* am the wizard here, thank you very much. Autoformat my heart? Force my soul into outline mode? I don't think so.

Many of PowerPoint's most vociferous critics suggest abandoning the software along with other restrictive technologies. I remember my colleague David Thornburg showing up to present at a Computer-Using Educators (CUE) conference with just a single long-stemmed red rose. Between his teeth, if I remember correctly. John Medina, in his delightfully informative book, *Brain Rules*, states quite simply that "professionals everywhere . . . need to do two things:

1. Burn their current PowerPoint presentations.

2. Make new ones." [8]

In this chapter, the plan is to adopt a conservative approach toward Medina's tongue-in-cheek exhortation. Rather than burning (or even deleting) our existing hard drive full of PowerPoints, let's start by pulling out a few slides and seeing if we can tweak them to achieve better results.

To achieve maximum impact with minimal effort, this chapter's tweak-easy slideshow fixes will focus on three categories: templates, color, and type.

Templates

Nancy Duarte, author of *slide:ology* and designer of the slides that Al Gore used in the movie *An Inconvenient Truth*, writes:

> You need to pry yourself away from the default templates with their preordained slide junk. Think through what is really required. What reflects your intent and personality? What will act in service to your information rather than compete with it? [9]

She continues: "Backgrounds are intended as a surface on which to place elements. They are not themselves a work of art. [They] should never compete with content." [10]

Presentation Zen [11] master Garr Reynolds warns against bombarding the viewer with irrelevant elements that distract rather than support the content that you are trying to display on the slide.

Activity 1.2

Identify what you might call distracting or noisy elements in this artist's rendition of a vintage, vendor-supplied template:

Where does the eye go first on the slide?

Does the *location* of that fluorescent dog kibble exacerbate the problem?

In English we read from left to right. The visual anchor, the decorative frou-frou, needs to be on the left.

And, yes, I know you can flip the canvas horizontally in PhotoShop. That draws the eye to the correct place on the screen, but, still, do you want the focus to be on those little fluorescent squares? What do they have to do with "Factoring Polynomials," "Cell Mitosis," or whatever other compelling subject is the topic of your presentation this class period?

Activity 1.3

Go through your archives and find a slide cluttered by a distracting template or background. Identify the specific elements that obfuscate rather than clarify your message.

Color

It's more than a little ironic that I'm sharing information about color with you here in black and white. Of course, you realize, we are operating within the constraints of print or, more precisely, the *cost* of printing in color versus black and white. The most economical way of including color in a printed book is to gather all the colored images into the center of the book. So, yes, for a more colorful discussion of this topic, please see Chapter Seven, which will be bathed in color. Also, check out the supplemental materials in color on the *They Snooze, You Lose* DVD that accompanies this book.

Color has a history of being expensive. Think back to paintings from the Middle Ages. The ultramarine blue pigment was originally made from ground-up lapis lazuli, a very expensive stone. Therefore, it was reserved for the most important person in a painting, such as the Virgin Mary. Other expensive colors were vermillion red (made from sulfur and mercury) and gold. They were used for holy figures or for wealthy patrons who could pay handsomely for their portraits.[12]

But now that digital color is essentially free, we modern-day Botticellis can afford to paint all our subjects in color. And for teachers and presenters, color is not only an aesthetic choice but also a pedagogical imperative. As the classic, widely quoted study sponsored by 3M at the University of Minnesota School of Management has quantified, there is dramatic improvement in audience comprehension and retention when black-and-white visuals are replaced with color.

1. Color visuals increase willingness to read by up to 80 percent.

2. Color boosts motivation and participation by up to 80 percent.

3. Color enhances learning and improves retention by more than 75 percent.

4. Using color in advertising outsells black and white by 88 percent![13]

Have any content you want to "sell"? Anything you'd like the audience to remember? What would *you* like to remember from what you've read here about the power of color?

Activity 1.4

What can you do to ensure that the black-and-white pages of this book will work for you? You guessed it! Pull out those yellow highlighters, sticky notes, and color flags. Reread the previous numbered list. Highlight your favorite statistic in yellow and tell someone why that particular fact would encourage you to use more color in your presentations.

Personally, I like point number three. I can't help thinking that buying each student one of those yellow markers with the built-in sticky flags would be a pretty economical way to raise test scores.

Why yellow? Of all the 16.7 million colors the human eye can see, it will go to yellow first. As color guru Carlton Wagner explains:

> The eye has an order in which it sees colors. Yellow, or colors with yellow dominating, such as lime green, are seen before others. When it comes to quick vision, there is no color seen faster than yellow.[14]

Activity 1.5

If you live near a museum with French Impressionist paintings, spend an afternoon with Claude Monet. Alternatively, mine the Internet for these three Monet paintings:

- *The Fisherman's House, at Varengeville (La Maison du pêcheur, Varengeville)*, 1882, Museum Boijmans van Beuningen, Rotterdam, Netherlands
- *Sunlight Effect Under the Poplars (Sous les Peupliers, effet de soleil)*, 1887, Staatsgalerie, Stuttgart, Germany
- *Antibes Seen from the Salis Gardens (Antibes vue de la Salis)*, 1888, Toledo Museum of Art, Toledo, Ohio

Make a list of the objects in blue and the objects in yellow. Which objects seem closer? Which seem farther away? Where does the eye go first? As the graphic artists say, which color "pops"?

What other colors grab attention? (Why have red pens been the preferred weapon of English teachers for decades?) Again, according to Wagner, it was initially believed that red was the fastest color seen, which explains why fire engines and other emergency equipment were painted red. In general, warm colors like reds and yellows are seen before cool colors like blue or green.[15]

Activity 1.6

If you were designing a presentation template, what would be the best color combination? Why?

	Background	Foreground/Text
1	Blue	Yellow
2	Yellow	Blue
3	Red	Green
4	Green	Red
5	Green	Yellow

If you chose yellow text on a blue background you have already got your Monet's worth from this book. (Skip to Chapter Six for more bad puns.) The eye goes to yellow before any other color. Blue, calming and evocative of pleasant natural elements such as water and sky, naturally recedes to the background.

If you chose number two or three—cool letters on a warm background—this would be a good time to do a little more research (beyond the scope of this book) on cool and warm colors.[16]

If you chose four—red letters on a green background—you may want to reconsider. About 8 percent of males have some type of color deficiency in their vision, with the most common problem being an inability to distinguish red from green.[17] For these men, your red words would just disappear into your green backgrounds, leaving them staring at a seemingly blank slide.

The fifth choice, which nature illustrates beautifully in every field of sunflowers, is yellow on a dark green. On the "Color Matters" website of J. L. Morton, we learn that green, universally accepted as symbolic of nature and freshness, is also the most restful color for the human eye. It has great healing power.[18] I feel better just thinking about it.

Of course, no matter how great the color combinations look on your computer screen at home, they may look terrible on the projected screen at your presentation venue. A recent experience brought this home to me. I was talking about the power of images to a group of media directors, enthusiastically describing my projected image of "Earthlights" (NASA's satellite view of the Earth at night). The audience was looking at me strangely and, finally, one person said: "Turn around." The whole screen was black! I lifted up my laptop and turned it around to show them the image. Fortunately, for that group, it was a two-day training and I was able to procure a different projector for the second day.

If you are consistently presenting in the same location with the same equipment, you can run some test slides with potential color combinations. If you are at the mercy of event managers—particularly ones who ask you how to spell 3LCD—it's better to err on the side of good contrast (such as yellow letters on a blue background) rather than experimenting with gradients or images that are particularly dark or low in contrast.

Edward Tufte, in his classic book *Envisioning Information*, begins his chapter on color by warning that the cardinal rule for tying color to information is *Above all, do no harm.* Beautiful colors that render information illegible are worse than no colors at all.[19]

And, I would add, beautiful colors that might offend your audience are worse still. Take blue and gold. Beautiful combination. Should be safe, right? Not if you are seated on the red and white Stanford side of the stadium during a football game against archrival University of California, Berkeley, whose uniforms are (you guessed it) blue and gold. A clueless Stanford freshman, on that chilly fall day I had worn my only pair of wool slacks (blue) and my winter coat (gold). My date quickly wrapped me in a red blanket, assuring me that rabid Stanford fans would strip anyone wearing an outfit as offensive as mine.

Because people react so immediately, so viscerally, to specific colors, color is a quick way to set the mood for your presentation. What colors are you using on your opening slide? (What does the audience see when entering the room?) What feelings will those colors arouse? Might the audience associate those colors with occurrences in the natural world? For example, red might evoke a sense of danger or heat because it reminds the audience of blood or fire. In addition, as Nancy Duarte points out, red might work for one industry (such as a blood bank) but not for another (such as a financial institution).[20] In any case, make sure your message and your palette are consistent. The beautiful blue template for your "Oceans of the World" presentation would make a strange backdrop for "Wildlife of the Kalahari."

Activity 1.7

Review this section and highlight keywords that prompt you to think of questions you should be asking yourself as you choose colors for a particular presentation. Flag one tip you can put into immediate practice and share with a colleague how you plan to use it.

If you would like to read more on the topic of color, you may wish to consult "Chapter Four: Color Power" from the author's award-winning book, *Visual Literacy: Learn to See, See to Learn*, published by the Association for Supervision and Curriculum Development (ASCD) and available in print or electronically on the website: www.educatebetter.org. By the way, in that same publication, Chapter Three is all about type, the subject of our next section.

Type

Regarding tweaks to type, there are two broad topics to cover: the sheer number of words per slide, and the typefaces, colors, and layout options used to display those words.

First, visual verbosity. Sounds like an oxymoron. Like an objective opinion or an original copy.

We've all suffered through slideshow presentations with line after line of text, reminiscent of the ghastly typed transparencies that speakers used to lay on the overhead projector, saying: "I know this is too small for those of you in the back to read."

Fortunately, most presenters have moved from transparencies to slides, from overheads to LCD projectors, but, unfortunately, many are using the new tools to continue the same bad practices. As John Medina likes to point out, the average PowerPoint slide contains forty words.[21] What about yours? How many words are crammed on your slides?

Activity 1.8

Boot up your laptop. Check out your last PowerPoint presentation. Jot down the number of words in each of six typical slides. Calculate the average. Write your average number here: _____

Activity 1.9

(Group activity) Get up from your seats. Line up by your average number from the most to the least slide-wordy person in the group.

Have the teacher represent John Medina with an average number of forty.

Starting from the highest number, count aloud, down the row. As each number is called out, feel free to disparage ("boo") the high numbers and applaud ("woo-hoo!") the low ones.

Group challenge and goal: By the end of the book, let's see if we can move John Medina to the top of the line! (Guaranteed, he would love this! Maybe we could send him before-and-after pictures?)

Note: A high-resolution version of the photo above, suitable for printing, is available with Medina's permission on the *They Snooze, You Lose* DVD.

How can we reduce the number of words on a slide? Could we use the Takahashi huge-text method[22] and limit ourselves to only one or two words per slide to guide the audience through the presentation?

I have not seen any slideshows outside Japan in which the presenter sustained the discipline of one to two words per slide throughout the presentation. An award-winning slideshow by Jeff Brenman[23] of Apollo Ideas on the world's water shortage comes the closest. To prepare the viewer for a litany of shocking ("Did you know?") statistics, an introductory slide displays a simple question mark, poignantly releasing a single droplet of water:

At the end, Brenman reprises the droplet and layers a single word:

As usual, Nancy Duarte gives the most practical (and doable) advice. She reminds us that presentations are a "glance media"—closely related to billboards. "Ask yourself," she writes, "whether your message can be processed effectively within three seconds"[24] (the time it would take to drive by a billboard).

More reading than that just sounds like too much work! I'm glad I sat in the back. I think I'll just check my email.

Quantity then quality

Once we have reduced the *number* of words on the slide, we still have to optimize the *display* of the words that remain. For me, an opportunity came last week to do just that.

My neighbor Dave heard that I was "good at that PowerPoint stuff" and asked if I could help him tweak his résumé before he posted it online. I said, "Sure, no problem," thinking it was a fifteen-minute project. Twelve hours later, I sat Dave down to go through the changes. He has graciously agreed to let me share three of the before and after slides with you in case you might identify with some of the befores and learn something from the afters. I changed Dave's last name and cell phone number to protect his identity but the rest of the facts are accurate representations. (The before and afters are included in full color as "Dave's Resume.ppt" on the *They Snooze, You Lose* DVD.)

Slide 1

Notice in Dave's original opening slide the stark white background glares on the screen. Almost all the words are in capital letters, which are difficult to read because with all the letters the same height, we have no ascenders or descenders to give us visual clues to speed up reading the text. To make the slide even less inviting, with the monochromatic text and lack of images, there is nothing visually appealing to draw in our attention or direct it around the screen.

On the revised slide, we started by tinting the background a light gray. The color is not dark enough to cause a problem if printing out the slide, yet it manages to add a subliminal richness while eliminating any unpleasant screen glare. We changed the typeface to Trebuchet, which is on everyone's computer. It's a clean, legible font—not too tightly kerned[25]—that's a bit softer than the straight-edged Helvetica or Arial. (Once we realized that the curvaceous Trebuchet *g* looked more like me than Dave, Dave decided to go back to Helvetica.) We put Dave's name in blue to make it stand out from the rest of the text and visually connect to the water behind the eagle, which, like Dave, also has an eagle eye, and is clearly skilled at getting the job done. Some Canadian friends just reminded me that the eagle does symbolize the United States (and Dave was proposing to help our citizens working overseas) and that they appreciated my spelling out CA to avoid any confusion with Canada!

Slide 2

On Dave's next slide, he again overused uppercase letters, making the text difficult to read. With all the text the same size and color, the eye doesn't know where to begin. And, if you have the tenacity to read down to the third bullet, it becomes apparent that it's not a third service but rather an explanation of the word *guidelines* in the second bullet. Plus every line is just a standard return after the line before it, giving no clue as to which lines belong together.

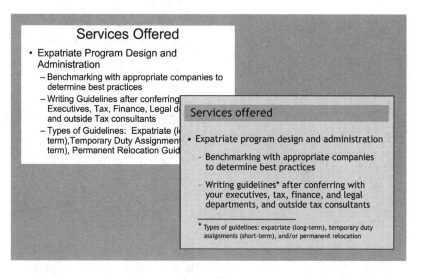

On the revised slide, the title is displayed in blue on a light blue box and left-justified at the top of the slide. The eye will go to color before it will go to black and white, so we can be assured the reader will see *Services offered* first and know immediately what to expect on the rest of the slide. Notice that only the first letter of the title is in uppercase, a practice now gaining widespread use because of the accelerated legibility. We also want the top line to start in the left-hand corner because the eye naturally scans from left to right, so finds it awkward to start in the center and then have to go back to the left for the next line. In the revised slide, look closely at how the leading (the space between the lines) is used to separate the bullet points and group the information into meaningful chunks. Finally, see how the guidelines information is relegated to a footnote, where it belongs.

Slide 3

Dave's closing slide did not take advantage of color (free on the Internet!) nor did it vary the leading to clump information on the slide. Everything is just dumped together and it takes awhile to figure out that there really are two distinct messages or thought groups on this slide:

- The first (scope and billing rates) says, "I'm flexible and would negotiate."

- The second (photo and email) says, "Contact me, please."

On the revised slide, we chunked the text into the two thought groups: the scope and price of services on the top and the contact information in the lower right-hand corner. We removed the hard-to-read underlines and instead used the blue accent color to highlight the key points. We deleted extraneous words such as "Contact." (Why else would he give you his phone number?) We added visual interest with a picture of Dave showing his smiling face, confirming he's the kind of pleasant fellow you'd feel safe having show up in your office as a consultant.

What can we learn from Dave's revised résumé? You may be more comfortable shooting a video and uploading it to YouTube than creating a PowerPoint résumé. But at least give it a try. Even if your résumé eventually ends up in some other format, thinking through the questions below can be a useful exercise:

- What product(s) and service(s) do you have to market and sell?

- What experience have you had that would make your customers confident that you could do the job? Do you have references from previous customers or employers?

- What would you charge? How can people contact you?

- Can you create a compelling image that represents your company's product(s) or service(s)? A smiling close-up of you (if relevant)?

- (Optional) Is there a sound track (music, other sounds) that would amplify your message? (This would have been counter-productive in Dave's case.)

Activity 1.10

Create a four-slide PowerPoint presentation that covers the following:

1. Name of company or product or service and compelling visual image (This is your grabber! No clipart. Clipart does not grab! It gags!)

2. Services you would offer (Why should they buy from you? Cheaper? Better?)

3. Relevant experience you've had, talents you have (What success stories can you document?)

4. Price sheet, your photo, and contact information (Close-up of smiling face)

Please use this activity to demonstrate your mastery of type and screen layout (as well as your hidden consulting prowess).

Which typeface did you select for your presentation? Is your text easy to read? Remember that

- Lowercase letters are faster to read.

- Widely kerned fonts (with generous space between the letters) such as Georgia and Verdana avoid collisions of letters on the screen.

Typeface	Font
Georgia	This font is 14-point regular.
Times New Roman	This font is 14-point regular.
Verdana	This font is 14-point regular.
Arial	This font is 14-point regular.

- Varying the leading (space between the lines) improves legibility and allows you to group your points to help the reader process the information visually.

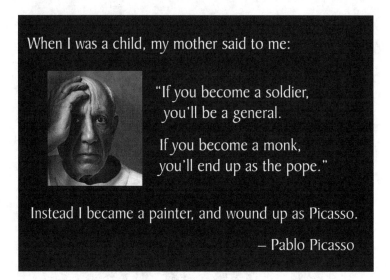

When I was a child, my mother said to me:

"If you become a soldier,
    you'll be a general.

If you become a monk,
    you'll end up as the pope."

Instead I became a painter, and wound up as Picasso.

— Pablo Picasso

- If presenting to a large group consider whether your font size is big enough so your text can be read from the back of the room. Use my little eye chart as a test:

18 point

24 point

36 point

48 point

60 point

During my live presentations, I ask for a volunteer—preferably a single male—sitting in the back to let me know which is the smallest line of type he can read. It's too late to change anything at that point but one can never do too much field research.

When preparing a presentation in the comfort of your home or office, you can approximate what the audience will see by reading your slides in the slide sorter view. And, as Nancy Duarte recommends, it works best if you set the view at 66 percent.[26]

- The typeface you selected should match your content. In my live trainings, I often show the following image:

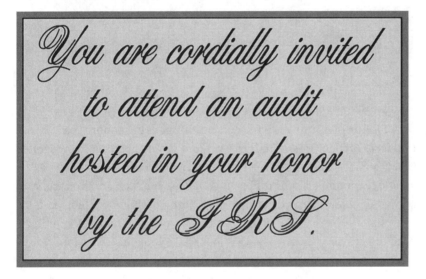

I ask the audience what was its first impression when it saw the invitation.[27] Most respond that they anticipated a wedding or a formal dinner party. Initially, few were able to decipher the swirling capital letters to realize the host would actually be the United States Treasury's Internal Revenue Service (IRS).

If this were a real communication from the IRS, the typeface would not be nearly as pretty. In fact, all IRS forms are set in Helvetica—the second-most commonly used typeface in the United States. It's perfect for the IRS: extremely legible, no serifs, no nonsense. But unless you want to be mistaken for the IRS, it may be wise to avoid Helvetica—particularly in sensitive times such as the first two weeks in April.

Did you use more than one typeface on your slides? Can you think of a situation when you would use sixty-nine different typefaces on one slide? To answer that question, have some fun with the following activity:

Activity 1.11

Take the ransom note below and change every letter to a different typeface. If you are so inclined, you may also add color and animation where appropriate.

Dear Customer,

If you have already paid the ransom,

please disregard this notice.

Note: This is more fun to do in a group so you can compare the wildly different creations.

The rule of thumb for presentations is not to have more than two typefaces on one slide: usually a serif font for the heading (more legible in larger sizes) and a sans serif font for any body text. The typefaces should harmonize but be different enough to not look as if you were trying to match them and almost did. (Think of that navy blue pullover that *almost* matches your navy blue slacks. Not pretty. Better to go with the gray slacks. At least that looks as if you chose both items on purpose.)

We know immediately, intuitively—in our gut—when a typeface is appropriate or inappropriate. If you had to pick a typeface to represent you, which one would you choose? Or would it vary depending on what you were trying to communicate?

Activity 1.12

Take a few moments today to design and write a thank-you note. Make the typeface an integral part of the message. Be conscious of the image your written words project. The recipient(s) may forget your words; they won't forget your (type)face.

Activity 1.13

Review one of your existing presentations in light of what you've learned in this chapter regarding templates, color, and type. Commit to one thing you can change, for sure, from now on in all your presentations. Write it down here:

_____

_____

List at least two more things you promise to try, at least once:

1. _____
2. _____

2

Creating slides and handouts

When someone asks me what I do for a living, I respond that I'm a *teacher* (followed by "I teach teachers to make better presentations."). People nod, give me a grateful smile, and usually groan about the last boring presentation they had to sit through.

Lately, okay just this afternoon (you can't rush these things), I've been thinking that we are probably even more impatient with sitting through thirty- to sixty-minute, linear, live presentations because we've grown used to prerecorded media where we can fast forward through anything we do not find amusing, entertaining, or immediately relevant.

On the web

Internet usability consultant Jakob Nielson warns that you only have about ten seconds to grab visitors' attention before they click off your site.[1] There is no charming presenter alongside to entice viewers to linger, no one to add clarification, change the sequence on the fly, or answer questions as they arise. This does not present a problem for purely *entertainment* presentations. A video of a cat playing the piano or a prairie dog staring into the camera probably needs no further commentary. For *edutainment* presentations, however, there needs to be enough information to at least *introduce* a more serious topic. That information can be delivered as limited text on the screen, as in Jim Bennan's award-winning slideshow *THIRST*[2] or as recorded voice-over narration, as in middle-school student Darian Coggan's HyperStudio production, *My Name is Cholera.*[3]

On the stage

In contrast to presentations posted on the Internet, *live* presentations—although they may also be well prepared and carefully scripted—offer the option of on-the-fly flexibility. Depending on audience response, the presenter may decide to skip a few lines, recount a different story, and attempt another joke . . . or not. The live presentations also fall into the same two broad categories as the posted ones: *entertainment* and *edutainment*.

For *entertainment*, we go to movies and plays, concerts and operas, and we don't expect to be tested on the content when we leave. As my friend Marian says, "Nobody but Lynell takes notes at the opera." Keynote presentations—particularly the variety delivered at statewide and national conferences—almost always fall into this entertainment category. The seductive speakers lure you into their world where you "catch" the contagious emotion they are sharing. In most cases, you can take two aspirin and be over it by the next morning. But a few find ways to keep the feelings alive. Bonnie St. John[4] is a good example. After her inspirational closing keynote at the Association for Supervision and Curriculum Development (ASCD) Conference in Chicago, she invited attendees to sign up for her free newsletter. Since then, I've had several email exchanges with her and am planning to attend a retreat she's holding at her place in the Catskills this summer.

For *edutainment*, we turn to classroom teachers (think the late Jaime Escalante), college professors (think John Medina), and professional developers everywhere who work tirelessly so that their students and attendees can learn. This is the category of presenter that I am primarily addressing in this book.

For this live presenter-edutainer-educator, the demands are rigorous. Not only do you need to be as engaging as a Bonnie St. John, but you also have to get across volumes of content and you are held *professionally* responsible for students remembering it on the test and *morally* responsible for their learning it well enough to apply it in new situations (after the test). In short, your audience has to laugh, cry, *and* learn. So, how do you make this happen?

For starters, you do *not* follow the standard slideshow procedure:

1. The presenter creates a series of *slides* with bulleted text.
2. The software automatically transforms the slides into *handouts*.
3. The *presenter* reads the slides to the audience.

Sadly, what masquerades as efficiency is just the opposite: a total waste of time. The problem is that under this standard procedure all three parts are essentially the same outline of text. It may be

1. Displayed
2. Printed out
3. Narrated aloud

but it's still just the same outline of text. What a waste of paper for the handout! What a waste of screen real estate for the display! What a waste of the potentially mesmerizing (as opposed to anesthetizing) personality of the presenter! And what a waste of time for the audience! (More than one person has asked: "Why didn't you just email me the handout?") As noted previously, about one billion people per day are bored blitzed by bullets! You may be saying, "No one ever died from boredom." One woman did tell me she was so bored by a Power-Point presentation that she prayed: "Lord, take me now!" But she lived to tell me about it, so to my knowledge there is no documented case of actual death by boredom from PowerPoint. But here's the critical point—especially for us educators: boredom and learning are mutually exclusive.[5]

On their heads

The solution—the last-ditch attempt at fixing boring slideshows—is to recognize that the problem is not the three aspects of a presentation themselves

1. Slides
2. Handouts
3. Presenter

The problem comes from making them redundant[6] rather than complementary[7] or synergistic.[8]

The job of the slides

What should you put on the slides? In most cases, what's too expensive to put on the printed handout—color, especially full-color, photographic images—and what's in your mind's eye but may not be obvious to your students or other audiences. Places they might not have been (How about Varkala Beach in Kerala, India?). Paintings they might not have seen (El Greco's *View of Toledo in a Storm*? Renoir's *Madame Charpentier with Her Children*?). Animals they might not have petted (wombats? meerkats? okapis?).

Activity 2.1

Try to recall a presentation that you gave or attended when the use of images made the presentation more effective. What do you remember about this presentation? Does any specific image come to mind? If so, why?

The most compelling evidence for using images comes from the body of research conducted by Richard E. Mayer and his colleagues at the University of California, Santa Barbara. Mayer's research confirms what good teachers have always known intuitively: The best way to foster learning involves *both* words *and* pictures.[9] The key is in knowing which goes where.

Activity 2.2

Which of the following slides do you think would be the most effective for learning?

National Oceanic and Atmospheric Administration
(NOAA) online photo gallery
NOAA's Ark collection of marine mammals
www.photolib.noaa.gov/animals/anim0215.htm

"Spotted seal – Phoca largha"
Image ID: anim0215, NOAA's Ark (Animals)
collection
Location: Bering Sea
Photo Date: May 1979
Photographer: Captain Budd Christman,
NOAA Corps

Online Photo Collections

National Oceanic and Atmospheric Administration
(NOAA) online photo gallery (20,000+ images)

NOAA's Ark
marine mammals

Is anyone drawn like a magnet to the all-text slide? What about the second slide, with its cute little photo and nicely laid-out text? That is an attractive slide, but because the eye goes to images before text, the audience will be looking at the picture and then start getting really frustrated because there may not be enough time to copy down all the words before the presenter moves on to the next slide. And besides, putting those words on the screen makes the presenter (who would be reading those words) redundant.

So, who voted for the third slide with the full-screen photographic image? That *is* the correct answer but this was a trick question.

If all I did, as the presenter, was show you gorgeous full-screen pho-tographic image after gorgeous full-screen photographic image, how would you have a clue what I was trying to communicate?

Instead, I show you the image (visual channel) and then tell you (auditory channel) about it. Classic show-and-tell. Your brain uses each channel for what it does best. Then intuitively, effortlessly, it integrates the two and delights in doing so.

How well does this dual channel, show-and-tell method work? What is the impact on recall and retention (think test scores) and trans-fer of learning (think using knowledge *after* the test)?[10]

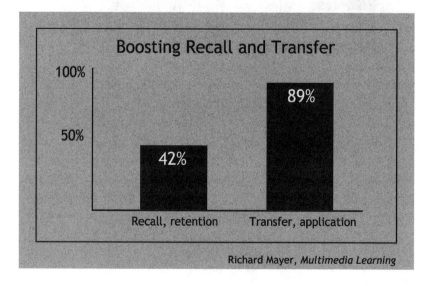

Given this research, plus over thirty years of experience teaching and presenting, I ask: Why would we present any other way?

Time to start organizing your slides in the Slide Sorter View rather than the Outline View. It's the photographic images that your audience is going to remember. The words are only empty frames until you insert the photographs.

Activity 2.3

In the Slide Sorter View, look at the last presentation you created. How many of the slides are full-screen photographic images? How many are screens of bulleted text?

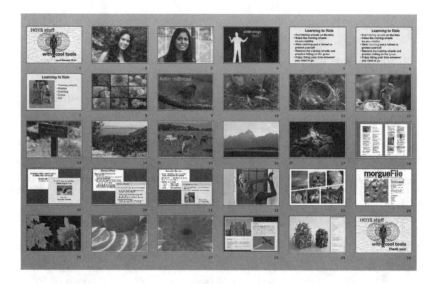

Activity 2.4

Revise your best (most visual) slideshow or work with a partner to create a new one with all full-screen images. Keep notes (in the Notes View) of keywords, references, quotes, URLs, and other information you will need for the handout.

So what goes on the handouts?

Take one of your favorite slideshows or the great slideshow you just created in Activity 2.4. Think about its gorgeous full-screen, full-color photographic images and the text pruned down to just the title of your presentation and the authors' names on the opening slide.

Remember that the handout *complements* rather than *replicates* the slides, so you can't just dump those slides into an auto-generated handout. If not thumbnails of the slides, then what *does* go on the handout? Every word you say when you narrate the slides? Absolutely not! That would make the handout or the presenter redundant rather than complementary. No, the handout has its own unique roles to play.

Black-and-white text

On the Slides	On the Handout
Color	Black-and-white
Photographs	Text

It makes sense to use each medium for what it does best: the electronic screen for the full-color photographic images and the paper handout for the visually boring black-and-white text that would be a waste of screen real estate.

References

If there are books, articles, websites, quotations you refer to during the presentation, put those on the handout. If scholars besides you have researched a particular topic, this is a good place to give them credit. (Besides, if you can prove that luminaries agree with you, your opinions will have more credibility. You'll notice me quoting Richard Mayer, John Medina, Garr Reynolds, Nancy Duarte, Roger Wagner, and other respected names in the field.) It doesn't make sense to have students or audience members sitting there copying (or miscopying) from the screen those names, quotations, or other long strings of text.

How long should the handout be?

One of the first hour-long presentations I did for a large conference audience was on the topic of Internet resources for K-3 reading. The handout was twenty-seven pages long and cost me $457 to duplicate at Kinko's. Just in case anyone reading this would miss the blindingly obvious, what I should have done was to print out one page, front and back, listing the sites I was going to demonstrate *during* the presentation and then refer the audience to the full twenty-seven-page electronic handout posted on my website to use *after* the presentation!

I want it *now*

So many presenters today open with, "The handout is on my website; I'll show you the URL at the end of the session," and then they give the audience nothing to refer to *during* the presentation. In these situations, I'm afraid I won't remember what I thought was important, so, instead of focusing on the presenter, I'm scrambling to write things down that are *probably* on the website. Don't misunderstand me. I definitely appreciate whatever the presenters want to post to complement what they are sharing during the session, but how exactly does that help me *now*? Couldn't they give me a one-page, double-sided handout that follows along with the presentation and where I could circle and underline things that I wanted to come back to after the session?

Lest you think I'm the only person who feels that way, I get a ton of positive comments from attendees about how much they appreciate my handouts, such as the one shown here from my spotlight presentation, "Technology Velcro," at the International Society for Technology in Education (ISTE) conference in Washington, D.C.

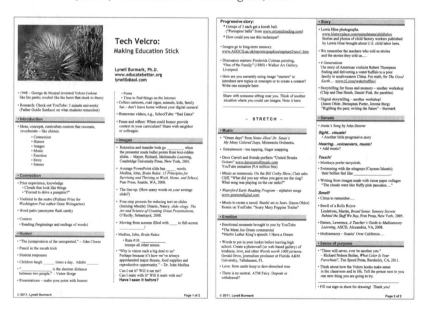

Notice that it is in two-column format (which allows you to get more onto a page) and has limited graphics (the opening slide graphic, to match the handout to the slideshow presentation) and the giveaways in the drawing, gray bars highlighting the major sections of the presentation, plenty of white space (margins and blanks) for writing notes, and URLs for linked sites, including where to download this handout as a .pdf or an editable Word document.

The online handout

So, you may ask, "If the presenter gave you the URL for the website at the *beginning* of the presentation, why would you need the handout printed out? Couldn't you just log on and follow the presentation from there? These days, everyone (with a charged battery) has wireless access!"

Why do you think the presenter doesn't do this? Have you tried presenting to a classroom or a ballroom full of people with their heads buried in their laptops? How is this different (that is, any less irritating) than a husband trying to talk to his wife when her head is buried in the morning newspaper? It's pretty clear in both of these cases that attention to the person trying to communicate has diminished because it has been divided.

We've always known intuitively that if you try to do two things at once, at least one suffers. Drinking and driving. Flying a kite during an electrical storm. Laughing and feeling sad.

But lately, some folks theorize, the human brain has evolved to the point where we, or at least the young among us, are now capable of multitasking. There is a lot of anecdotal evidence that appears to support that theory. Personally, I've had face-to-face conversations with my niece Shanta while she was texting one friend, on Facebook with another, and—she assured me—completing a homework assignment with two other classmates. I've watched in awe while my nephew Tor contributed to multiple online discussions while composing a new song on his guitar!

But more recently, as John Medina explains, "The best you can say is that people who appear to be good at multitasking actually have good working memories, capable of paying attention to several inputs *one at a time.*"[11]

Medina continues: Studies show that a person who is interrupted takes 50 percent longer to accomplish a task. Not only that, he or she makes up to 50 percent more errors.[12]

Some people, particularly younger people, are more adept at task-*switching.* If a person is familiar with the task, the completion time and errors are much less than if the tasks are unfamiliar. Still, taking your sequential brain into a multitasking environment can be like trying to put your right foot into your left shoe.[13] There is still that brief moment of "Now, where was I?"—that need to refocus attention—that occurs every time a person switches gears. The example in the media spotlight now is texting or talking on a cell phone, activities that Oprah's January 21, 2010, episode—"America's New Deadly Obsession"—informed millions of fans were as dangerous as driving your car after having four drinks![14]

So what does this mean for classroom or ballroom presentations? If students or audience members are buried in their smart phones and their laptops, then are presenters like designated drivers trying to speak sense to a room full of drunks? There's probably a nicer way to put it but essentially we have to admit that the tech-savvy students and attendees are not—as they would have us believe—actually multitasking. Every time they click on that laptop or text on that phone they are choosing to disconnect from the teacher-presenter. We are doing our best to communicate with a group of twenty to two thousand people and each one is in essence asking twenty to thirty times during our fifty-minute presentation, "May I put you on hold?" and then not waiting for our permission to do so.

Think of those times when you have to phone tech support, an insurance company claims department, or just about any company's "customer relations." How long do you stay on hold before you just hang up? What's the point of even trying to give a presentation in that kind of disconnected environment?

It may be, as some pundits are currently arguing, that the traditional stand-and-deliver presentation is coming to the end of its natural life span. (Ironically, most of those pundits are still making their living standing up and delivering that message on stages around the world.) I would agree with them that the combination of a talking-head presenter and a buried-head audience is not going to work for the long term.

For the short term, I think the best approach for those brief lectures during the school day (or those short sessions where the educator-edutainer-presenter is delivering content at a conference) is to establish a no-phone, no-laptop zone. We can promise resources on a blog or website and use the smart phones and laptops to build learning as a part of other activities, but during the actual presentation, as they say on the airlines, "all electronic devices must be turned off and stowed!"

Activity 2.5

How do you feel about cell phones and online computer access during a classroom lecture or conference presentation? If you are in a setting to do so, stage a debate between students, colleagues, or conference attendees. Give a teacher-presenter the chance to comment on the best arguments from each side.

Although it goes beyond the purview of this book, I cannot help wondering if this attempt at multitasking isn't part of a problem much bigger than smart phones and laptops. When we try to do two things at the same time, neither is savored. As Eckhart Tolle expresses it: "You are never fully here because you are always busy trying to get elsewhere."[15] It is only when "you make the present moment, instead of past and future, the focal point of your life [that] your ability to enjoy what you do—and with it the quality of your life—increases dramatically."[16] When you focus that joy on a goal, "there will be enormous intensity and energy behind what you do. You will feel like an arrow that is moving towards the target—and enjoying the journey."[17] We miss not only the joy but also any chance to soar in this life when we try to gain time by interrupting the flight of the arrow.

What about the words?

Early in my brief tenure as the director of education for a projector reseller company, my CEO came to see me work with a group of educators. As we were leaving the event, he said to me somewhat incredulously: "You *talk* like those people." I had to laugh. We educators do have our buzzwords!

We can assume that Eckhart Tolle would not be impressed by our educational jargon. He warns:

> Words can cast an almost hypnotic spell upon you. You easily lose yourself in them, become hypnotized into implicitly believing that when you have attached a word to something, you know what it is. The fact is: You don't know what it is. You have only covered up the mystery with a label. The

3

Celebrating presenters

Apple Computer CEO and world-class presenter Steve Jobs loves to use the phrase *insanely great* to describe new products that Apple is releasing. I love the energy and enthusiasm in that phrase and think it will be perfect to describe *you* as a presenter by the end of this chapter!

Let's start by looking at three broad categories of presenters to see where you fit in and then let's discuss some specific tips and strategies to fine-tune your presenter attitude, preparation, and delivery.

1. **The lecturer** presents us with mind-numbing instruction that results in disengagement (example: *Ferris Bueller's Day Off* [1986]). Facing a dazed and dosing classroom—minus Matthew Broderick as student Ferris Bueller (who took the day off)—the high school economics teacher, played brilliantly by actor Ben Stein, droned through a lecture peppered only by the question: "Anyone? Anyone?" to which only he responded:

   "In 1930, the Republican-controlled House of Representatives, in an effort to alleviate the effects of the . . . Anyone? Anyone? . . . the Great Depression, passed the . . . Anyone? Anyone? The tariff bill? The Hawley-Smoot Tariff Act? Which, anyone? Raised or lowered? . . . raised tariffs in an effort to collect more revenue for the federal government. Did it work? Anyone?" and so on.

dream. As Bill Clinton says: "He has the gift to inspire." *The New York Times* calls him "the high priest of human potential."[5]

Activity 3.3

Who else fits in the motivational speaker category? Maybe some computer evangelists? Diet and fitness gurus? Conference keynote speakers?

Write down your best examples with a brief explanation of what makes the presenter effective.

Do you see parts of yourself in any one of these three categories? Which one of these types would make the best presenter for an audience of educators or a classroom of students? Religious preference, musical taste, and guru druthers aside, which celebrity would you rather have present or perform at your next conference or teach your class for the day? If they would come for free, would you want Billy Graham, Cher, Céline Dion, Tony Robbins, or . . . ?

I was going to say, "or all of them?" However, that particular foursome probably doesn't golf on the same course too often.

But what if we could take the best of what we just described from all of them and combine that into one super presenter-performer? What if we created a fourth category and called it . . .

4. **The educator** empowers students to retain and transfer learning. (Of course, the "students" can be teachers or kids or anyone placed in a situation primarily intended for learning.) Rather than singling out one model educator as an example of this category, I'd like to offer two complementary examples—one from a film and one, well, I don't want to spoil the surprise.

In the first example, the Warner Brothers movie *Pay It Forward*, twelve-year-old schoolboy Trevor McKinney (Haley Joel Osment) is given a class project to complete by his social studies teacher, Eugene Simonet (Kevin Spacey). Trevor's task is to figure out a way to change the world through direct action. He comes up with the plan to "pay it forward" by doing a good deed for three people who must in turn each do good deeds for three other people, creating a charitable pyramid scheme.

3

Celebrating presenters

Apple Computer CEO and world-class presenter Steve Jobs loves to use the phrase *insanely great* to describe new products that Apple is releasing. I love the energy and enthusiasm in that phrase and think it will be perfect to describe *you* as a presenter by the end of this chapter!

Let's start by looking at three broad categories of presenters to see where you fit in and then let's discuss some specific tips and strategies to fine-tune your presenter attitude, preparation, and delivery.

1. **The lecturer** presents us with mind-numbing instruction that results in disengagement (example: *Ferris Bueller's Day Off* [1986]). Facing a dazed and dosing classroom—minus Matthew Broderick as student Ferris Bueller (who took the day off)—the high school economics teacher, played brilliantly by actor Ben Stein, droned through a lecture peppered only by the question: "Anyone? Anyone?" to which only he responded:

   "In 1930, the Republican-controlled House of Representatives, in an effort to alleviate the effects of the . . . Anyone? Anyone? . . . the Great Depression, passed the . . . Anyone? Anyone? The tariff bill? The Hawley-Smoot Tariff Act? Which, anyone? Raised or lowered? . . . raised tariffs in an effort to collect more revenue for the federal government. Did it work? Anyone?" and so on.

Activity 3.1

Come up with other examples of presentations that would fall in this "lecturer" category. Make a list of characteristics that these presenters share. Then create a composite, fictitious presenter who lectures and completely loses his audience in the process.

If you are working in groups, transform your ideas into a humorous skit to perform for the rest of the class.

If working independently, make a list of things an ineffective lecturer in your subject area might do. Keep that as a reference guide so that when you are creating and delivering your presentations you can avoid those pitfalls!

Of course, the lecturer *can* be like the high school economics teacher in *Ferris Bueller's Day Off.* But the lecturer could *also* be like one of the TEDTalk presenters,[1] or like veteran evangelist Billy Graham. Consider how Graham not only kept his lectures (sermons) short, but he also warmed up his audiences with music and joined hands with local churches to follow up with all the crusade converts to give them the tools and the support they needed to grow in their newly found faith. As of 2008, the lifetime audience for Graham's crusades, including radio and television broadcasts, topped 2.2 billion.[2]

2. **The entertainer** offers delightfully mind-numbing performances that result in escapism (example: *Cher: Live in Concert from Las Vegas* [2010]). With more than a dozen new Bob Mackie costumes, the beat goes on. Have a few drinks in the intimate setting of Caesars Palace, relax, and enjoy the show! Thinking subsides. You forget all your problems as you start singing along with vintage classics like "Believe," "I Got You Babe," and "Gypsies, Tramps & Thieves." Mind-numbingly entertaining but, as Eckhart Tolle warns: "There is a high price to pay" for this "spirited" state. "Instead of rising above thought [into a state of awareness and heightened Being], you have fallen below it."[3]

Similarly, the problem with passively watching television or full-length educational films is that the longer you focus your attention on the screen, the more your thought activity becomes suspended.[4] You relax and escape from your problems but you quite literally lose your mind in the process.

Activity 3.2

What can a classroom teacher (or live presenter) do to encourage active participation during films or longer video clips?

What role do the students (or audience members) play in making the performances relevant or empowering?

In most cases, the entertainer generally has a sense of what the fans like but doesn't know the members of the audience as individuals and rarely has any personal contact with them. Céline Dion, for example, became a household name with her exquisite rendition of "My Heart Will Go On," theme song of the blockbuster movie *Titanic*. She's been singing to sell-out crowds in Las Vegas for over a decade and her CDs have sold around the globe. But what impact has she had beyond bringing beautiful music into people's lives? On a recent *Oprah* show when Céline was the guest star, a young lady skyped in from England to tell Céline that it was through her song lyrics she had learned about love and how to be a better person. The young lady had grown up in a series of abusive foster homes and had no positive role models in her life—other than Céline. For that young lady, who is now teaching love to others as a wife and a mother, Céline was a very effective mentor. And thanks to Oprah, Céline got to see that.

3. **The motivational speaker** inspires us and has an impact, short or long term (example: Tony Robbins: *The Ultimate Edge* [2010]). Yes, Tony Robbins is the man who popularized walking on fire— 2,000-degree-Fahrenheit hot coals—as an activity to demonstrate that it's possible for people to do things that seem impossible to them. Obviously, Tony Robbins has done more than walking on coals. Millions of people think he also walks on water. But there again his actual performances are only part of his course that includes individualized components and ongoing guidance for participants to achieve the dreams that Tony has helped them

dream. As Bill Clinton says: "He has the gift to inspire." *The New York Times* calls him "the high priest of human potential."[5]

Activity 3.3

Who else fits in the motivational speaker category? Maybe some computer evangelists? Diet and fitness gurus? Conference keynote speakers?

Write down your best examples with a brief explanation of what makes the presenter effective.

Do you see parts of yourself in any one of these three categories? Which one of these types would make the best presenter for an audience of educators or a classroom of students? Religious preference, musical taste, and guru druthers aside, which celebrity would you rather have present or perform at your next conference or teach your class for the day? If they would come for free, would you want Billy Graham, Cher, Céline Dion, Tony Robbins, or . . . ?

I was going to say, "or all of them?" However, that particular foursome probably doesn't golf on the same course too often.

But what if we could take the best of what we just described from all of them and combine that into one super presenter-performer? What if we created a fourth category and called it . . .

4. **The educator** empowers students to retain and transfer learning. (Of course, the "students" can be teachers or kids or anyone placed in a situation primarily intended for learning.) Rather than singling out one model educator as an example of this category, I'd like to offer two complementary examples—one from a film and one, well, I don't want to spoil the surprise.

In the first example, the Warner Brothers movie *Pay It Forward*, twelve-year-old schoolboy Trevor McKinney (Haley Joel Osment) is given a class project to complete by his social studies teacher, Eugene Simonet (Kevin Spacey). Trevor's task is to figure out a way to change the world through direct action. He comes up with the plan to "pay it forward" by doing a good deed for three people who must in turn each do good deeds for three other people, creating a charitable pyramid scheme.

Applying this concept to the world of educational presentations, if a presentation were truly empowering, then attendees should be able to adapt the contents into their own presentations and lessons for (at least three) other people. I'm christening this the Teach It Forward (TIF) plan.

What if you are in the classroom? One zero-budget way to reduce class size is to have the students TIF. You, the teacher, present a chunk of content to eight students. Each of them reteaches it to three others. You end up with eight empowered teaching assistants and a total of thirty-two students who have nailed the content. You pick eight different students for the next chunk.

What if you are giving the keynote in front of 2,500 attendees at an education conference? A perfect opportunity to reach at least ten thousand educators if everyone agrees to TIF.

In other words, present the content in such a way as to empower the audience (be it educators or students at any grade level) not only to *retain* the content but also to be able to *transfer* it into new situations and to other individuals. Unless they pass it on, their knowledge pool becomes stagnant. Actually, this is one of the great privileges of being an educator: we get to *share* the things we are most passionate about. That's one reason why our profession is referred to more often as a *calling* than as a *job*.

Speaking of jobs, are you ready for the second example? The CEO of Apple Computer.

You may not have thought of Steve Jobs as an "educator," but he is certainly recognized as one of the best presenters on the world stage. A Steve Jobs presentation combines *lecture* that informs, *entertainment* that captivates, and *motivation* that inspires. If you have not seen him live, catch one of the over 68,700 clips of his presentations currently posted on YouTube. If you are still not convinced that he'd make an awesome professor, read *The Presentation Secrets of Steve Jobs: How To Be Insanely Great in Front of Any Audience*, by *BusinessWeek* columnist Carmine Gallo.[6]

My tongue is a little in my cheek (okay, hard-wired) on this one because I do understand that no professional educator has Jobs's staff or time or budget to create a presentation. But the ten tips I've listed below (cherry-picked from Gallo's analysis) are free for the mimicking and among the best strategies that I've already been advocating as applicable in an educational setting.

10 Tips from Steve Jobs	
1	Have fun.
2	Toss the script.
3	Use your body.
4	Pause for effect.
5	Dress appropriately.
6	Change it up.
7	Provide a headline.
8	Do the preparation.
9	Be the presentation.
10	Present what you love!

Steve Jobs has spent decades making this list (and more) look easy. For the average educational presenter (or the students we teach), tackling all ten tips at once would be daunting if not totally overwhelming. What I would propose instead would be to conduct a self-assessment to establish a baseline and then, as you plan new presentations, pick two or three skills to focus on for that presentation.

Activity 3.4

Give yourself a score of 1 to 10 points for each skill:

___ 1. *Have fun.* Do you look forward to giving presentations? Do you smile often (and even laugh!) while presenting?

___ 2. *Toss the script.* Do you talk to the slides or the audience? Do you read from notes, the handout, or the screens or do you converse with audience members or students as if they were friends just sitting across the table?

Activity 3.4 (cont.)

___ 3. *Use your body.* Do you make eye contact with the audience, have open posture (no lectern), and use expressive gestures?

___ 4. *Pause for effect.* When you make a key point, do you take time to let it sink in or do you race to cover the next thing on your agenda?

___ 5. *Dress appropriately.* Do you set an example with your wardrobe—dressing a little better than everyone else but not in ways that the audience would find distracting? (Sorry, as Gallo warns, no blue jeans until "you invent a product that can change the world."[7])

___ 6. *Change it up.* Are you a talking head for more than ten minutes at a stretch? Or do you share the spotlight with other experts, shift to different media, and engage audience members in activities and make them co-presenters?

___ 7. *Provide a headline.* Do you express the essence of your presentation from the audience's perspective, providing a pithy quote to forward as a text message?

___ 8. *Do the preparation.* Do you spend the time to research the topic, organize your ideas, and find compelling images, video clips, and stories to illustrate your key points?

___ 9. *Be the presentation.* Although you may not be as equated with your content as Steve Jobs is with Apple Computer, can you get into it credibly and convincingly?

___ 10. *Present what you love!* Even if you're the football coach assigned to teach one period of U.S. History, can you dust off the old adage, "If you can't be with the one you love, love the one you're with"? Can you look for the good—for the lovable, if you will—in the course or topic you are assigned to present? Can you tap into a genuine passion for your message?

Add up your scores _____ and divide by ten ___ for one quick assessment of your current presentation prowess. Date ___/___/___ and keep the score sheet as an encouraging reminder of what you already do well and of techniques you might want to hone as you develop new presentations.

Activity 3.5

If you are working independently, focus on adding one more strategy, when you feel comfortable, with each new presentation.

If you are in a class, work in groups of three to six people to create a short presentation (five to six slides) incorporating at least three of the ten tips. Choose one person to deliver your presentation to the rest of the class. Your grade for this activity will be based on how many of the ten strategies the other classmates can identify. (Anything over three counts as extra credit!)

If you are a classroom teacher, think about how you could use these tips to transform assignments that students used to turn in as written reports or read as bullet points from traditional, text-laden Power-Points. Particularly at the lower grade levels, you could start with short, three-slide presentations so the preparation wouldn't be overwhelming.

One example that comes to mind is the annual bird unit my niece Shaila does with her second-graders in Tigard, Oregon. Each student gets to pick one bird to report on. I had the privilege last year of working with one of Shaila's students to do his research on the robin redbreast. When we found a website with great images and he saw that *his* bird laid *blue* eggs, he was beside himself with excitement. His three slides could be

1. *Title slide:* "robin redbreast" and "John B." (only words in presentation) over image showing bright red breast and habitat

2. *Favorite food:* worms (mmmmm, yummy)

3. *Unique fact:* blue eggs!

I guarantee—especially after the rest of the class gasps when it sees the full-screen, full-color, projected image of the blue eggs—that fifty years from now Johnny will still remember those eggs. And so will every other student in that class!

The students shouldn't need a script for just three slides. After doing the research, these kids really get passionate about their birds! And even second-graders can learn to pause for effect: "And the unique thing about *my* bird is that it has . . . (click to slide 3) *blue* eggs!"

Having fun, tossing the script, pausing for effect, doing the preparation, and presenting what you love with the flair of a Steve Jobs? Not bad for a second-grader!

If you haven't already highlighted them, make a commitment to focus on number one (have fun) and number ten (present what you love). It's no accident that the first and last tips are both about attitude. When those two steps are positive, you and your students can and will master all ten.

Activity 3.6

Practice smiling (a jump-start on skill number one). Put a pencil in your mouth horizontally (see the picture), like a smile extender, securing it with your teeth. Turn to someone beside you; exchange smiles. Turn the other way, to another person; exchange smiles. If you are working independently, find the nearest mirror and smile at yourself until it hurts your cheeks or you feel your mood lifting—whichever happens first.

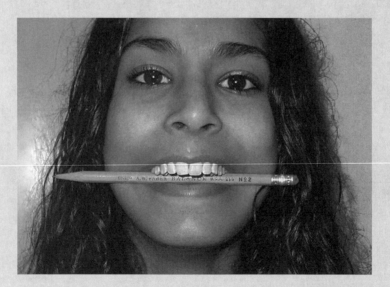

Next time you are working on a presentation, consider using the smiley pencil trick for inspiration. If you are smiling when you are creating the presentation, your audience will feel that smile when you deliver it!

Another issue to consider is how the audience's interests affect the success of the presenter. For celebrities, this is easy. The audience self-selects based on the reputation of the presenter. When Steve Jobs presents at Macworld people stand in line for hours outside Moscone Center in San Francisco to get the front-row seats. They hang on to every word and photo-capture every slide.

For those of us who have not yet achieved Jobs's level of fame, how do we make sure the people who could get the most from what we have to offer are the ones coming to our presentations? At conferences I've found that my catchier titles in the program entice the most people:

- "Learn to Read or Go to Jail: The Imperative for Early Literacy"

- "Making Education Stick: Veni, Vidi, Velcro! (I Came, I Saw, It Stuck!)"

- "Enlighten Up! An Educator's Guide to Stress-Free Living"[8]

For on-site trainings, I'm especially impressed with the system that colleague Jim Brazell[9] deploys to make sure his content will meet the wants and needs of his clients. About three months before each scheduled event, Jim sends a form with five questions that at least three different individuals or groups from the client organization have to fill out and send back to him. He uses their responses to tailor his presentations and "*play*shops." (With Jim, even though participants accomplish amazing feats, nothing feels like *work*.)

Activity 3.7

For a conference session, what would you like to know about your audience enough ahead of time to help plan your presentation?

In the classroom, what kinds of information could or should you gather about students before planning a lesson or presentation?

What about when you are already standing there, starting your presentation? Is it too late to tailor the presentation content to the audience? Not if you are Howard Pitler, technology guru and senior director for curriculum and instruction at McREL (the Mid-continent Research for Education and Learning center where Bob Marzano and others do such great work). At the 2010 ASCD conference in San Antonio, Texas, Howard conducted a two-hour workshop on using technology to support the nine teaching strategies that Marzano has documented to work in schools. Howard took a poll to see which *two* of the nine strategies he should address. (He would have needed *days*, not *hours* to cover all nine.) To keep everybody happy, Howard offered additional resources for all nine, so attendees could pursue their individual interests after the session.

What about adapting your presentation to the audience's learning styles? A technique that I've used is to hang eight posters in the presentation room or classroom. As participants or students enter, they are given a handful of sticky dots and told to affix those to the phrases that best describe how they learn.

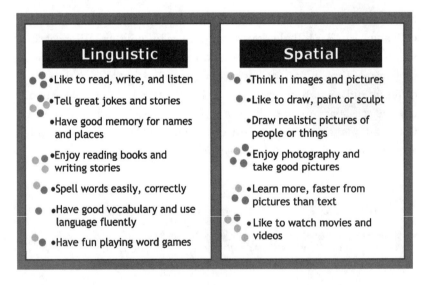

Note: Make sure to laminate[10] all the posters so after the event you can just peel off the sticky dots and have the posters to reuse the next time.

With all eight of Howard Gardner's multiple intelligences[11] represented—linguistic, logical/mathematical, spatial, bodily-kinesthetic, musical, interpersonal, intrapersonal, and naturalist—you get a quick picture of the proclivities of your group members. Do they prefer to learn from pictures (spatial) or words (linguistic)? Do they like to get up and move around, stretch, or maybe even dance (bodily-kinesthetic)? Do they need more reflective cave time (intrapersonal) or more time working in triads (interpersonal)? Are they like the group I worked with in Buffalo, Wyoming, that placed 80 percent of its sticky dots on the naturalist poster? The distribution of the dots will quickly answer all those questions.

Then, what do you do with that information? The naturalist leanings of the group in Buffalo—which should not have surprised me given the breathtaking beauty of the location nestled at the foot of the snow-capped Big Horn Mountains—were a bit of a challenge for me, given that my idea of the great outdoors is the atrium at the Hyatt Regency. But at the very least, I could have and should have taken or downloaded some nature photos from the area and worked those into my slideshow.

A good presenter will already be tapping into the multiple intelligences in every session but the presentation needs to be flexible enough to weight activities and delivery modes to audience preferences as they become known. For example, are you providing time for the intrapersonal learner to contemplate and process new information before exchanging thoughts with others? Are you facilitating the interpersonal learner's style by providing opportunities to "share something you learned in the last ten minutes with the person next to you"?

Activity 3.8

What could you do (differently) with a group that put 80 percent of its sticky dots on the bodily-kinesthetic chart? If feasible, stand up, stretch, and discuss this with two other people. Prepare to share your best ideas with the larger group.

If you're home alone reading this, stand up, walk to a mirror and—with great passion and enthusiasm—tell yourself three things you could do to make your presentations more physical. If it helps, start by singing Olivia Newton John's classic pop hit "Let's Get Physical." "Let me hear your body talk . . ."

Time for a quick assessment. Put the pencil back between your teeth (the enlightened way to take tests).

Question 1: Now that you are smiling, do you remember our earlier discussion in Chapter Two about full-screen photographic images? Can you see how adding voice-over narration to the images (show and tell) would boost recall and retention?

Answer 1: Smile. Nod. 10 points.

Question 2: Do you recall discussion in Chapter Two about getting a perfect ten on your handouts? Can you see the handout as the place "where you transform what I think is important for you to learn into what you think is important for you to remember"?

Answer 2: Smile. Nod. Another 10 points.

Question 3: Can you see yourself—besides excelling as a lecturer, entertainer, and motivator—eventually mastering all ten of Jobs's presentation tips?

Answer 3: Smile. Nod. 10 more points.

So, with the multiplicative effect ($10 \times 10 \times 10$), your score is 1,000. Yes, 1,000 is the new 100. Yes, you're that good.

Yes, this applause is for you and your insanely great presentation. Hands are clapping in gratitude for the hard work you put into your slides and the rich handout that you are making available for your audience members to adapt and enhance with the ideas you sparked in them. The standing ovation is showing appreciation for the contagious passion, caring, and humor you poured out as you delivered the presentation.

So, take a bow and smile. Smile at all those wonderful people who have learned from you and who will, with their own smiling faces, Teach It Forward.

PART 2

Revolution

In case you missed the news, a revolution has occurred. Silently. Bloodlessly. But irrefutably. Yes, the locus of control has transferred from what the teacher-presenter intends to impart to what the student-audience chooses to remember.

So, how can we help our students, our audiences make the right choices? How can we influence what they retain? What will "stick" their whole life long?

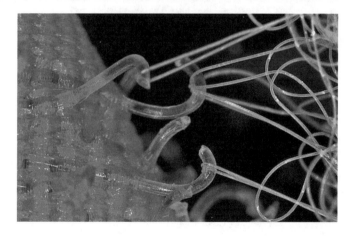

Think Velcro. It's as simple as connecting our hooks to their loops.

Come now and exercise your gray cells and your laughing muscles, celebrate the ways you are already making your presentations memorable, and discover additional hooks and lots of fun activities to connect attendees to your awesome content and make all your presentations seductively "sticky"!

4

Ringing
CHIMES[2]

One of my favorite sessions to present—"K–12 Education in Five Minutes or Less"—was inspired by a timeless sketch from *Saturday Night Live* laureate Father Guido Sarducci. (Type the words *5 minute university* into YouTube to access the video.) In the four-minute clip, the comedic priest explains to a group of empathetic college students that in *his* university the entire degree program takes only five minutes. In his Spanish class, for example, you learn the question *¿Cómo está usted?* (How are you?) and the response *Muy bien, graçias.* (Very fine, thank you.) No time to learn vocabulary and conjugations and "all that junk." Because five years after you graduate, Father Sarducci contends, *¿Cómo está usted? Muy bien, graçias,* is about all you're going to remember. So, at his university, that's all you learn.

Of course, he is a comedian. But serious educational pundits are starting to relay the same message, seemingly oblivious to the irony in their words. For example, Larry Ainsworth wrote a book titled *Power Standards*[1] in which he admits that no teacher has time to cover *all* the standards so he just expounds on a few of them—the really important ones.

Standards über guru Robert Marzano admits that to cover *all* the standards students would have to go to school K–22,[2] and that some of the instructional strategies he has documented as most effective should be "limited to crucial content" because they are too time-consuming.[3]

Then there's my dental hygienist, the self-appointed Floss Fairy who, in my opinion, says it best: "You don't have to floss all your teeth. Just the ones you want to keep." Think of all the drill and kill we do as educators. What prioritization skills can we learn from Father Sarducci, Larry Ainsworth, Robert Marzano, and the Floss Fairy?

Consider one simple example: teaching students how to type. The current system? After practice, practice, and more practice, we give the students a five-minute test. We look over their work until we find the fifth typing error. Then we stop, count the words up to that point, and divide by five to get a words-per-minute score. We do this assessment ritual twenty or thirty times (once for each student in the class). Is anyone having fun yet? Who really cares how *fast* you can type? Isn't it more important just to be *accurate*? So, the Father Sarducci typing test? Cover the students' hands and keyboard with a dishtowel. Have them type their name. If it's correct they pass.

Activity 4.1

Think of a topic or skill you are currently teaching. Brainstorm ways to present or assess it more efficiently. Share your idea with someone else in sixty seconds or less. Use a merciful dose of humor to keep the audience awake. A minute is a long time to have to pay attention to one speaker.

Did I really just say, "A minute is a long time"? Unfortunately, I'm not alone in wanting to speed things up. A quick 0.31-second search on Google for "one minute" just returned 368,000,000 hits! We want everything from our morning oatmeal to our evening Hot Pockets to be done in sixty seconds or less. Moreover, in the context of educational presentations, we need things not only to be *done*, but also *well done*. We need *efficiency* (how *fast* you can teach it) to meet with *effectiveness* (how *well* they will learn it).

To be *effective*, we need to accomplish two things:

1. Get their attention.

2. Make the presentation stick.

The first challenge is exacerbated by the fact that we live in a "culture of distraction" and suffer from the "information-fatigue syndrome" of modern life.[4] To illustrate this, Dr. Edward Hallowell, a psychiatrist who specializes in attention deficit disorder (ADD), suggests the following activity:[5]

Activity 4.2

Take a pen, pencil, or marker in each hand and put a piece of paper on a flat writing surface in front of you. Make sure you are seated comfortably. Proceed to draw a triangle with your left hand and a square with your right hand while tracing circles with one foot (your choice).

Now, I would suggest, add an electronic device—your choice—to the juggling act. (So much for technology making our lives easier.)

At this point—keep juggling!—which of the following teacher-presenter approaches would be most apt to get your attention:

1. Announcing that "the way a presenter dresses can either help bring home a point or just distract the audience."

2. Showing up with pink hair and matching pink feather boa.

My walking up on stage dressed like this for last year's National School Boards Association's Technology and Learning (NSBA T+L) Conference elicited a whole range of reactions including the following:

- "I thought, 'Thank God. This presentation won't be as boring as the last one!'"

- "I didn't know they made Barbie outfits in adult sizes!"

- "Even after you changed into the navy blue suit, I couldn't get the image of that pink boa out of my mind."

Did I get their attention? Oh, yes. Especially the guy with the cell phone camera in the fourth row. But would I wear this outfit again? Probably not. It helped me make my point about how a presenter should (or shouldn't) dress but it distracted at least some of the audience members from other, more important points that I wanted to make. Perhaps the rule should be to *attract* but not *distract*. Sometimes there's a fine line. Sometimes there's a six-foot boa.

Activity 4.3

Share a time when you (or someone you observed) successfully grabbed the attention of a class or audience.

As you listen to others' humorous, visual, visceral, dramatic, and engaging antics, make a note of the ones that resonate with you, ones in which you could close your eyes and imagine yourself performing that technique.

So, now that you've experienced the first part of being an effective presenter (*getting* their attention), how do you accomplish the second part (*keeping* their attention) long enough to make your presentation stick?

That's where the Velcro comes in.

As history records it, Swiss engineer George de Mestral got the idea for Velcro one fine day in 1941 after returning home from a hunting trip in the Alps with his dog. He examined the burrs of burdock that had stuck to his clothing and his dog's fur.

Noticing (under a microscope) that the hundreds of burdock burrs looked like "hooks" that caught on anything with a "loop," Mestral envisioned the possibility of creating a fastener by joining together two materials that could replicate the hooks and loops. He named his invention *velcro*, a portmanteau[6] of the two French words *velours* (like his plush velour pants) and *crochet* (like the hooks of the burrs).

Activity 4.4

We might say that the primary job of educators is "to transform today's hooks into tomorrow's loops."

Think about what is meant by this metaphor. What are the hooks? What are the loops? Who does the hooking? Who's becoming increasingly loopy? If you are in a group, share your team's thoughts in an open forum in which group members can continue to add ideas as they are developed.

In order to begin answering the questions in this activity, let's start with a look at some hooks.

To create a context for that investigation, log on to YouTube and type in *Susan Boyle, singer, "Britain's Got Talent," 2009.* Turn up the volume and lose yourself in this most exquisite experience. Had you seen this video before? What elements make it work? Make it memorable? What hooks tug at your heartstrings (your heart loops, as it were)?

Activity 4.5

Think about how each of the following hooks played out in the "Britain's Got Talent" video and write down your answers to the questions. If you are in a group, discuss your answers with the rest of the team:

Connections: In what ways did we feel connected to Susan Boyle? Could we recall similar experiences when we might have prejudged people and underestimated their potential?

Humor: What made you laugh while watching the video? How did the laughter contribute to your overall enjoyment of and engagement with the performance?

Images: What role did the visual aspects play in the drama? How was Susan Boyle's physical appearance a factor? What was communicated by the facial expressions and body language of the judges? Of the members of the audience?

Activity 4.5 (cont.)

Music: Everything else aside, how did the music make you feel? What messages did the lyrics convey? Was this a good song choice for Susan? Did you believe she was singing from the heart? From visceral experience?

Emotion: List as many emotions as you can that you witnessed or experienced during the video.

Story: If the camera had just started recording when Susan began to sing, would the performance have been as powerful? How did her personal story—and the reactions of the audience and judges—add to the experience?

Senses: Was this a multisensory experience? How would it have been different if you had closed your eyes? Shut your ears?

Much as I dislike acronyms (they seem like the final, life-leeching step in reducing visions to images, images to words, and words to letters), I have to admit that I fell prey to mild delight when I noticed the hooks in the previous activity above created the acronym CHIMES[2].

I love the way chimes reverberate, echoing their mellifluous resonant frequencies, radiating them in every direction. I'm sure there are more chimes—probably at least a carillon—but for the purposes of our educational presentations, if we can learn to play even seven in our live performances, our audience members will synch up to the rhythm like toes tapping and hands clapping at a country-western concert in Nashville.

At this point, you might be thinking that you may not have the time to hit on all the chimes during this quarter or semester (or during this crazy, busy time in your life). There is no magic—other than the musical acronym—to the order of the hooks, so you can pick a few now and learn about the others later. Each of the chapters that follows describes one of the hooks in detail. In deciding which chapter (which hook) to select, students might find it helpful to use Dick Bolles's *Prioritizing Grid*, which appears each year in his ten-million-copy best-seller *What Color Is Your Parachute? A Practical Manual for Job-Hunters and Career-Changers.*[7] When Dick's readers and students use this grid throughout his "Flower Exercise," it helps them figure out what's most important, next most important, and so on. I have reproduced it here, with Dick's permission, to help us evaluate which hooks we find the most interesting or consider ourselves best prepared or most skilled to start using.

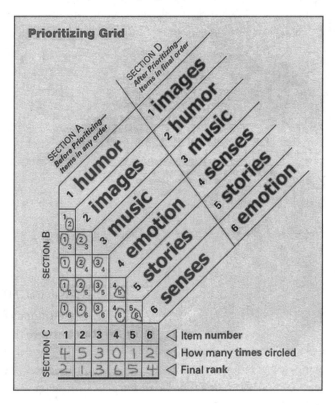

You will notice that I ranked the hooks according to my degree of preparation and comfort level using (and promoting) them in my live presentations.

In Section B, I circled my choices. Forced to choose between images 2 and humor 1, I circled images 2, and so on.

In Section C, I totaled the number of times I had circled humor 1 (four times), images 2 (five times), and so on. Then, based on the number of times circled, I entered the final rank.

In Section D, I wrote in the hooks in order according to their final rank.

Activity 4.6

Start with the chime or hook that interests you the most and read the corresponding chapter. Highlight at least three things you can do differently, two different (new) things you can try, and one resource or idea you can recommend to a friend or colleague.

If you are reading this book for a class, form a team with other members of the class who have chosen the same chime or hook. If there are too many (more than three) people on your team, break into multiple teams, subdivide the chapter, and decide which parts of the material each team will cover. Prepare a ten-minute presentation to deliver to the rest of the class. Schedule an additional two minutes for questions and comments from the audience.

Your grade for the presentation will be based on how well you

1. Grabbed and maintained the attention of the rest of the class

2. Modeled the hook you were describing

3. Gave the other class members replicable strategies and free resources to implement your hook

Remember to smile as you prepare and deliver your presentation because true joy is contagious. And also remember that your message only has value if you can hook the rest of the class into learning it well enough to Teach It Forward.

Making connections

Imagine that you are a math teacher charged with conveying the concept of *ratio* to a class of middle-school students whose favorite FAQ is, "Why do we have to learn this?"

Instead of launching into a one-sided tirade of abstract mathematical formulas or assigning three pages of decontextualized problems from the state-adopted math textbook, what if you showed a three-minute animation about something any teenager could relate to—a series of really bad dates?

Activity 5.1

Watch the hilarious little video "Bad Dates" on SchoolTube or download a copy from its creators at New Mexico State University.[1]

Like many dating hopefuls, the young woman in the video just wants "to find a guy who can speak to [her] on a one-to-one ratio."

Pedagogically speaking, the video creators have taken an abstract mathematical concept (ratios) and connected it to a concrete, real-world situation (restaurant dates with verbose, taciturn, and complementary conversationalists).

Making the abstract concrete

It's the concreteness that helps us understand. As authors Chip and Dan Heath put it: "Trying to teach an abstract principle without concrete foundations is like trying to start a house by building a roof in the air."[2] In this simile, series of lessons or presentations work to construct (the "house" of) knowledge over time and subsequently serve to support higher, more abstract insights (the "roof").

This makes perfect sense for an ongoing, multisession professional development class or a three-unit college course, but what about a one-shot presentation such as your two-hour workshop at your favorite annual conference?

For tips on delivering one-shots, there is arguably no better mentor than successful high-stakes presenter David S. Rose. David is a "pitch coach" who gives priceless advice to entrepreneurs making start-up-funding-request presentations to venture capitalists and angel investors. After a fifteen-minute "pitch," the entrepreneurs leave with either a "sorry" or a check for fifteen million dollars. So, David argues, after a dramatic and memorable opening "it is crucial that . . . the presenter immediately set out the context for the rest of the presentation. [Like] the scene on the outside of a jigsaw puzzle box, [the context] gives the audience the overall picture into which they can then fit each piece as you deliver it."[3]

Activity 5.2

At first, these two similes seem contradictory. The Heath brothers say you can't build the roof without a foundation and Rose says, in essence, that unless you show people the roof, no one will know where the foundation goes.

Look up the definitions for inductive and deductive reasoning. Which one matches which metaphor?

What do both metaphors argue must come first—the concrete or the abstract?

Either way—to build the roof or complete the puzzle—ideas in a concrete context are easier to remember. "If you've got to teach an idea to a room full of people, and you aren't certain what they know, concreteness is the only safe language."[4]

You can illustrate this point as follows:

- Ask the audience members to make a picture in their head when you say the word *rose*. Wait six or seven seconds.

- Show a slide with just the word *rose*. Wait another two or three seconds.

- Show a slide with a clipart image of a rose. Ask the audience, "How many of you had *this* image in your mind's eye?"

Offer condolences and let the audience know there is counseling available for clipart addiction.

- Show a slide with a full-screen, full-color photographic image of a beautiful pink rose in full bloom. Ask the audience, "How many of you saw *exactly* this? I mean, in your mind's eye, before I showed it to you?"

If you wanted everyone to see the real rose, what would be the best way to make that happen (besides passing around an actual rose, of course)? If you say the word *rose*, how many in the audience picture the clipart rose? A photograph of a rose? A different-colored rose? A bud? A vase? Aunt Rose? There is a continuum from the word (most abstract) to the rose (concrete) that you can examine with your senses. The more senses (sight, smell, touch) you engage, the more concrete the experience. (For more on engaging the senses, see Chapter Eleven.)

Activity 5.3

Choose something you are currently teaching and think of ways to present it more concretely. If you are working in a group, share your ideas with the others and have them make some suggestions as well.

One of the best applications of this principle is the *This Is Your Life* budget simulation created by Wes Burmark, my favorite brother and the director of technology for the Tacoma Public Schools in Tacoma, Washington. Instead of teaching spreadsheets as a generic tool, Wes has participants draw cards (as you would in a board game) for income categories (job, additional income, chance, savings) and expenses (house and car payments, food base + $75 per child, utilities, and additional expenses) and enter that information into the "Monthly Budget Worksheet." What makes the activity memorable is not the technical prowess of Excel but the twists and turns of life that lead to a person's trying to feed four children while making minimum wage at the local Dairy Queen. The most fun was when Wes ran the simulation with fourth-grade students. Their reactions were priceless:

- "Now I know why my parents are in such a bad mood the night they sit down to pay bills."

- "When I grow up, I'm not having any kids. They're too expensive to feed."

- "No way you can drive a Corvette and work at Dairy Queen."

Another concrete strategy comes from Tanisha Brooks, a middle-school science teacher at the Oliver Wendell Holmes Foundation Academy in Flint, Michigan. To teach classification, Tanisha takes her students out to the cement playground, where she draws a twenty-foot-wide Venn diagram with two overlapping circles. Visually surveying her *female* students (for whom the daily "outfit" is a huge deal), she comes up with labels for the two outer circles (for example, leggings and pink tops) and then has her *male* students direct the girls where to stand. (Girls wearing leggings *and* pink tops would be in the overlapping center part of the circle.) After a couple of rounds of this *concrete* game, the subsequent indoor, more *abstract* science classification Venn diagram becomes a no-brainer.

Building on prior knowledge

The classroom teacher has an advantage over the one-shot presenter in that an ongoing course provides more time to assess and build foundational knowledge before continuing to the next step. Of course, in today's high-tech world, both classroom teachers and presenters can use "clicker" systems that allow the audience to "vote" anonymously on questions to quickly reveal their preferences or levels of expertise or understanding. But one-shot presenters have little or no time to course-correct, so they either have to be certain of the audience's prior knowledge or, as David Rose recommends, "require no prior knowledge on the part of the audience . . . [and be ready] to answer every potential question at exactly the right place, just before the audience would think to ask it."[5]

In less pressured situations, when your presentation is not limited to fifteen minutes, you can have fun with the audience or classroom members by conducting on-the-fly prior knowledge assessments. (Part of the reason for doing this is to model the fact that not all assessments have to be painful paper-and-pencil tests.) Here are a few of the activities that I use:

- **Clouds that look like things**

    Download images from the "Clouds That Look Like Things" page of the Cloud Appreciation Society's website[6] and insert them into a slideshow. As you project the cloud images, audience members can recognize familiar shapes such as waves, a heart, a pipe, a rabbit, and so on. People will be smiling because the brain loves to make these kinds of connections. Make sure to point out how this feels more like a game than a test.

- **Humor with recall**

  Did you hear about the papa rat interrogating his two sons: "Turned into white horses? Home after midnight and that's the best story you can come up with?" What prior knowledge makes these questions funny?[7]

- **Sequencing historical events**

  Divide the screen into quadrants and fill each quadrant with a color image of a particular historical event. (I often use the Crusades, the Vikings, Christopher Columbus, and Lewis and Clark.) Divide into groups of three and have each group determine the chronological sequence[8] of the events depicted in the pictures. It's always interesting to see how much participants learn from talking with their peers and how adamantly they get involved in the discussion.

  The sequencing could also work for putting activities such as daily routines in order. Imagine "drilling" reflexive verbs in French class by using three photos of an age-appropriate young woman: brushing teeth, waking up, and combing hair. The teacher asks "What is she doing?" (*Que fait-elle?*) A student with a laser pointer indicates the sequence as the rest of the class responds: *Elle se réveille. Elle se brosse les dents. Elle se peigne les cheveux.*

Activity 5.4

Design other slides with three to six images. One possibility would be to time-sort electronic devices: record player, transistor radio, cassette tape player, palmtop, personal CD/DVD player, iPod, and so on. This can also be a group activity.

- **Digital flash cards (for example, antonym word pairs)**

  Start with a slide with one word in the top half of the projected image, for example, *up*. Once the audience guesses the opposite word (*down*), reveal it on the slide. Similarly, the next slide might have *in* and then *out*. For the third slide, try something that could have different antonyms depending on the context: *single* and then *double* (ice cream) or *married* or any number of humorous descriptors for the married condition.

  Note: For the screen version of the flash cards, I used light text on a dark background because it's easier to view as a projected image. For the typeface, I chose 220-point Verdana bold so the letters would have enough weight to be seen easily from the back of a classroom or ballroom.

  After two or three sample slides are shared, who creates the rest of these digital flash cards? (*Hint:* Who needs to learn these words?)

Activity 5.5

Brainstorm other digital flash cards you might have students or audience members create to pair up related bits of information for different grade levels and subject areas.

The digital flash cards can have *images* as well as *words*. For example, preschool and second-language teachers can find delightful illustrations for all the basic spatial concepts on the Meddybemps web-site at www.meddybemps.com/9.600.html. More pairs of opposites are illustrated at www.meddybemps.com/Opposites/HotCold.html.

Sometimes students surprise us with connections they make to prior knowledge. For example, when I visited Grimmer Elementary School in the Fremont Unified School District (Fremont, California), I was pleased to see a poster of the Mona Lisa in Maïda Cardenas' first-grade classroom but I had to chuckle when Maïda told me that her students thought it was a portrait of the Mexican painter Frida Kahlo. The maestra had shared her passion for Kahlo's art with her students, even to the point of displaying her favorite socks with an image of Frida Kahlo woven into the fabric:

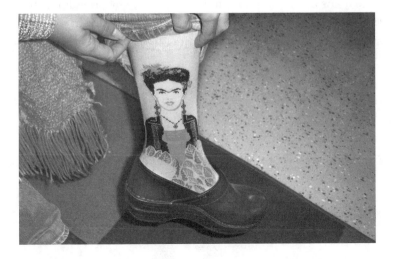

As John Medina explains in *Brain Rules,* the brain wants to know "where have I seen this before?"[9]

What we pay attention to and our emotional response to it are "often profoundly influenced by memory. In everyday life, we use previous experience to predict where we should pay attention."[10]

And "different environments create different expectations."[11] This explains the shock of one of my elementary school students running into me in the supermarket and exclaiming: "You eat?"

It also explains the incident of the violinist in the subway. If you'd like to watch the two- to three-minute clip on YouTube, just type in *Stop and Hear the Music.* Then imagine that you are in the subway station, on your way to work in the middle of morning rush hour. Against the wall, beside a trash basket, a youngish man in jeans and a T-shirt is playing classical music on the violin. Will you stop and listen? Will you throw a dollar or two into the open case at his feet? He seems pretty good. Do you have time to savor something beautiful or are you already running late for work?

Were you able to see beyond the humble trappings to recognize violinist Joshua Bell and his three-hundred-year-old, $3.5 million Stradivarius? Did you realize that, three days before, Bell had performed in Boston's Symphony Hall, where the cheap seats cost $100? Or were you on your cell phone trying to talk over the "noise"? Or perhaps humming along to some pop tune on your iPod?[12]

Prejudice is an ugly word and incidents like Joshua Bell's receiving only thirty-some dollars for his forty-three minutes of playing just exacerbate its bad reputation. However, it's only by prejudging, by sorting incoming data into predetermined categories that we are able to organize the overwhelming amount of information that barrages us daily.

10:2

In an educational setting, when new information is coming in, the time must be allocated for that judging and sorting process to occur on a conscious level.

Back in Maïda Cardenas' classroom (and every other classroom at Grimmer Elementary School), after each ten-minute chunk of teacher-driven content, students pause for two minutes of discussion with a partner. The school calls this "10:2" and classrooms observe the practice almost religiously. The pauses are programmed into the instruction and occur with nearly clock-like precision. Depending on the content and objective of the lesson, the direction for the two minutes will vary. Besides the generic "Tell the person next to you something that you didn't know ten minutes ago," the first-grade teacher might say: "Share where you've seen an animal like this before or where you think you might go to find one." "What other objects do you see in the classroom that are red?" "What do you wear to school that's different on a day when it's raining? Why?" "When have you or your parents returned something to a store? Why did you return it?" Or any number of other topic-related, open-ended questions to drive the content deeper and make it more personally relevant.

The 10:2 practice aligns pedagogically with John Medina's research findings that all students start tuning out after ten minutes of lecture.[13] The beauty of the Grimmer practice, in my opinion, is that it not only changes the pace to refocus kids after ten minutes, but it also allocates the time for students to make and articulate connections between the new learning and their expanding trove of prior knowledge.

My advice to teachers and presenters, preachers and entertainers? The 10:2 works in every venue with every type of audience. Go for it!

Compare and contrast

One of the best ways to introduce the connection process is to suggest comparing and contrasting. In his classic research opus, *Classroom Instruction That Works,* Robert Marzano identified nine categories of instructional strategies that are most likely to improve student achievement across all content areas and grade levels. At the top of the chart, the *most* effective strategy is "identifying similarities and differences."[14]

Traditional PowerPoint slideshows have not been the best means of supporting this strategy because they display images one slide after another rather than placing them side by side, which would have required using two projectors and two screens. (I'll never forget the look on one tech director's face when he had just finished installing two thousand Epson LCD projectors and I told him he needed a *second* one in every classroom!) Fortunately, before he started down that path, Epson introduced its new line of WXGA projectors. Instead of the old XGA resolution (1024 pixels wide by 768 pixels high, in the 4:3 aspect ratio of our traditional television sets), WXGA-projected images are 1280 pixels wide by 800 pixels high (in the 16:10 aspect ratio of HDTV).

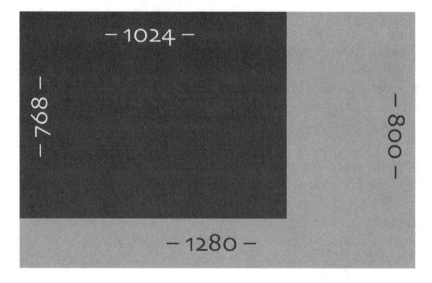

With 30 percent more screen real estate, you can juxtapose images side by side, project Venn diagrams, and plug items into nice, wide classification charts. Art teachers love the option of comparing two paintings (for example, same artist at different periods in his life; two different artists depicting the same subject or location); science teachers love software that supports recognizing patterns and dragging items into appropriate circles and boxes.

The wider screen is also useful when it comes to juxtaposing life's most fundamental choices:

Visually comparing the two options makes it easier to choose the better system. Just to make sure, you can add a bit of relevant research in support of your preference (for example, those who use the "overs" make an average of $32,000 more per year[15]). Anticipatory roll-changing also gives you the upper hand if your roommate does not share your penchant.

Did you know that Google currently lists over thirteen million postings regarding "over or under toilet paper"? Come on. Just give it up; it's "over."

Where everybody knows your name

Of course, searches on the great toilet paper debate cannot compare to the 535 million hits generated by the word *names*. Apparently a lot of people want to know what their name means and where it comes from. Names are a big part of any person's identity. Look at the movie stars and the melodious names they choose to represent themselves. My personal favorite is Angelina Jolie (French for "pretty little angel"). Then there are the iconic folks whose first name suffices to identify them: Prince, Cher, and, well, do you remember the television sitcom set in a Boston bar? And its theme song whose famous refrain—"Where everybody knows your name"—became the show's tagline? The running gag on the show was when patron Norm Peterson (George Wendt) would enter the bar and say "Afternoon, everybody!" and all the customers would shout back, in unison: *"Norm!"*

Sure, Norm came to Cheers for the beer, especially because bartender Sam Malone (Ted Danson) was willing to put it on Norm's tab for all eleven years of the series. (By the final episode, Norm's bar tab was so enormous that Sam had to have it calculated by NASA.) But the sense of belonging, of everybody knowing his name, also had to be part of the attraction.

What about in an educational setting? How powerful is it to know students' names? When Scott Lane Elementary School in Santa Clara, California, identified sixty-seven kindergartners who needed serious intervention for reading, principal Steve Kay hung their photos on his office wall and labeled each photo with the student's first and last name. These kids were not numbers. Everyone in the school knew all of them and greeted them by name. A thousand days later, by the end of second grade, sixty-five of the sixty-seven were reading at or above grade level.

What about coordinating with your art teachers to create a poster introducing each student? Consider implementing the wonderful project called Photo Expansion that begins with a photo of each child's head and trunk.[16] (The face is the hardest part to draw and it's imperative that everyone be able to recognize the child.)

Then have the students "expand" or complete the images by drawing the rest of their body into a poster that also depicts something they
enjoy doing. Put each child's name along the bottom of the photo frame
to help everyone put the name to the person.

Activity 5.6

Think about how you might use the Photo Expansion activity. Elementary
school teachers, where would you display the posters? Secondary teachers,
how could you do this with all 150 students who pass through your classroom
daily? Teacher trainers and online instructors, how might you make this into a
homework assignment? What hardware and software might you use to make
these posters into a slideshow or animated video?

Brainstorm other techniques you've used, observed, or considered for learning and using students' names.

School has been called the place where we can level the playing field, giving every child an opportunity. School can also be the place where students feel they belong, where "everybody knows your name."

In a one-shot, "drive-by" live presentation, knowing the names of everyone in the audience is more of a challenge. I did once witness a guest speaker at church who had all 450 members of the congregation introduce themselves and then he went back around and repeated all 450 of our names. I'm embarrassed to say that I don't remember *his* name.

Activity 5.7

At a districtwide professional development training or at a conference you've attended, what are some of the techniques you've used or observed other presenters employ to learn and use the names of people in the audience?

In my large-venue presentations, I've had audience members ask probing questions, offer insightful comments, and crack me up with their hilarious take on whatever I'm presenting. To honor their contributions, I make a point of acknowledging them by name when I repeat their words (over the microphone) for the rest of the audience.

Recently, in my spotlight session at the ISTE conference in Denver, I decided to take acknowledgments to the next level. I started asking my attendees to jot down their ideas and pass them to me along with their email address and permission to quote them in my next book or presentation.

For example, one of the learning tools I shared was the free online application Wordle, which creates word clouds where the size of words is determined by the frequency with which those words appear in the imported text. When I showed my Wordle Wordle (the Wordle that colleague Eric Dahm[17] created from my online Wordle article[18]),

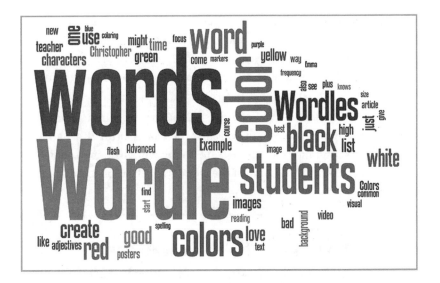

it scored big on the wow factor. But it only went from *wow* to *now* (as in *"Now* something I can use!") when Dustin Blaha, the technology staff development coordinator for the Rapid City, South Dakota, school district, suggested Wordle-ing your text as a way of identifying the "keywords" that you must make sure to illustrate with examples and images.

I reinforced Dustin's suggestion of illustrating keywords with this simple Colors Wordle:

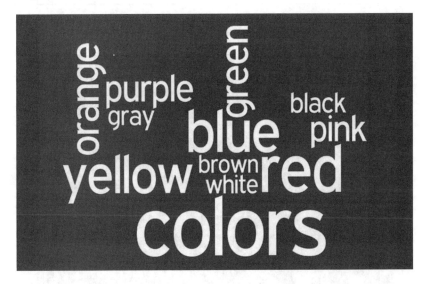

Once this image is inserted into your slideshow, you can embed links to full-screen, full-color photographic images from each color. (Clicking on red, for example, takes you to photos of red roses, a stop sign, a fire engine, and a red Corvette, or alternatively, for Texas audiences, a bright red truck.)

Then I explained how you could use the Advanced feature in Wordle to manually, intentionally *weight* the words as an alternative to importing text and having the program do the weighting by frequency of occurrence. Weighting some of the wonderful characteristics of my little friend Emma, for example,

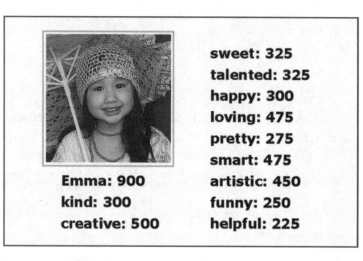

sweet: 325
talented: 325
happy: 300
loving: 475
pretty: 275
smart: 475
artistic: 450
funny: 250
helpful: 225

Emma: 900
kind: 300
creative: 500

produced the following Wordle:

Seeing the Emma poster,[19] another attendee at the presentation, Susan Freymiller, the head librarian at Culver Academies in Culver, Indiana, got the idea to have students create Wordles from autobiographies they had written.

That started me thinking about visual representations of students' future autobiographies—the description of what they want their lives to be five to seven years from now. As world-renowned clinical neuroscientist Daniel Amen, MD, has written in *Change Your Brain, Change Your Life*,[20] if you express your desired future in the present tense and study it every day, you end up creating that future. George Johnson, founder and ringmaster of TEL•A•VISION, has helped underperforming students weave images, music, and animation into videos that envision a better future. Students watch their videos over and over again, sixty to seventy times, and teachers are able to use them for behavior modification. ("How is your behavior helping you get what you want?") The videos also provide a foundation for forging motivated Individualized Education Plans (IEPs). George shares that at-risk students who saw no reason to stay in school, let alone consider college, are suddenly studying hard because a college degree is required for the profession they want to practice.

Consider the Wordle as an alternative or complementary way of organizing or capturing the keywords of the future each student is claiming. Words like *Harvard University, doctor, parent, healthy, homeowner,* and *joyful* could appear in the Wordle and be linked to images, music, and animation that would etch the future into long-term memory.

What could have been a five-minute demonstration of the free Wordle tool ended up—thanks to Dustin, Susan, Daniel, and George—transforming a cool tech application into a means of changing lives and making schools into places that help students visualize and get the skills they need to realize their dreams.

Connect

What about the physical connection between the presenter and the audience? You've been there. The keynote is staged in a large auditorium with fixed, raked seating like a movie theater. Every seat is filled except for the front four rows. The presenter is perched up on the elevated stage with her microphone and computer tethered to a switchbox another ten feet back from the audience.

Such was the setup for my back-to-back presentations at a media educators' conference in Spokane, Washington. After the first session, where I struggled for ninety minutes to project across all that empty space, I walked to the back of the theater where my eleven-year-old niece Jordan was passing out the handouts for the second session. I told her that all that empty space sucked the life out of me so to please ask the next group of attendees to come down to the front.

For the next fifteen minutes, educator after educator dutifully marched down and filled up the front rows of seats. I had never seen anything quite like it so I went back to ask Jordan what she was saying to the attendees. She replied, matter-of-factly: "I told them that it sucks the life out of the presenter when they sit in the back, so they'd better go down front."

When Jordan isn't available (that is, whenever the conference isn't in Spokane), I am forced to resort to blatant bribery. Everybody always gets a mini (one-inch-diameter) porcupine ball to use for an activity later in the presentation.

But if you are willing to sit in one of the first four rows?

Help yourself to a jumbo (three-inch-diameter), soft and slimy worm ball! Of course, yours to keep. You're welcome. ($14.95 for two dozen. Oriental Trading Company [www.orientaltrading.com].)

Of course, the bribes, er, uh, freebies support critical points in the presentation. No gratuitous party favors. That's one reason I always do a serious segment on chocolate in my "You Fill Up My Senses" presentations. Not that chocolate could ever be considered gratuitous.

Activity 5.8

Think of a presentation in which you could give away relevant freebies. Peruse a catalog or website such as www.orientaltrading.com for ideas.

On a tight budget? Sometimes the perfect freebies are lying in your own backyard. I still have the little pebble Pastor Steve gave each of us to hold when facing life's challenges: a pebble about the size of the one David used to bring down Goliath.

Pastor Steve also sits down with the children as he tells them a story before sending them off to children's church. For us adults, he uses a see-through, acrylic lectern rather than those imposing solid wood podiums that shielded medieval priests and modern ministers from all the sinners down in the pews. I have yet to see a transparent podium at an education conference. Maybe we need to add that to our list of AV requests?

As for getting down close to the audience, one of the most memorable "presentations" I've ever attended was a concert at the beautiful Flint Center at De Anza College in Cupertino, California. While waiting for the performance to begin, my friends and I noticed a guy seated a few rows over playing the saxophone. He was very good. A few bars later, he stood up and continued playing as he—Kenny G!—made his way onto the stage.

I keep thinking I'd like to pull a Kenny G next time I have a workshop in which the participants are seated six to a round table. I could have an activity posted on the screen with a note: "The presenter will be here momentarily. In the meantime, please . . ." And then I could sit at one of the tables and do that activity as a participant.

Activity 5.9

In your presentation venues, what can you do to get physically closer to your attendees? Brainstorm with others to make a list.

Breaking the language barrier

Of course, there is more to connecting to an audience than physical proximity. What if the audience speaks a different language than the presenter? Sometimes, it's just a "vehicular dialect." A couple of years ago, I was doing presentations in the northeast corner of Texas. It was immediately apparent that I was "not from here." Out of respect for the audience members, I asked them to be sure to let me know if I said or showed anything that didn't resonate with them. A few minutes later, when I was discussing the power of color in presentations, I showed my slide of a red Corvette to illustrate the passion and danger implied by that color. A woman in the first row crooked her finger and motioned for me to come close so she could inform me: "We don't drive Corvettes. We drive tru-ucks."

Three weeks later, I did a similar presentation at a Pearson Executive Forum in San Diego, California. My client offered to give me a ride to the airport afterwards and arranged to meet me in the hotel's parking garage. When I asked what kind of car I should be looking for, she said: "The one in your slideshow."

Another "not from here" experience involved a more serious language discrepancy. I had been presenting for about five minutes to a politely attentive but totally nonresponsive audience when I happened to give an example in Spanish. All of a sudden, the group came alive. Turns out none of the audience spoke English, a fact that the person who hired me had neglected to mention.

Activity 5.10

Ask a second-language teacher in your school for two or three examples of effective pedagogy for delivering instruction across language barriers. Consider how some of their techniques could be used to communicate new vocabulary or concepts to your own students even if they all speak your native language. Share your replicable findings with other teachers in your school or class.

Using humor to connect

As comedian Victor Borge asserts, "Laughter is the shortest distance between two people."[21] I'm reminded of this on Sundays when I get the giggles every time a certain teenage boy comes down the center aisle passing the offering plate. It's not the *collection* that's humorous, but the *recollection* of this young man's skit two summers ago at church camp that continues to crack me up and makes me feel as if I know him. In the skit, disguised as Little Bunny Foo Foo, he went

> Hopping through the forest
> Scooping up the field mice
> And bopping them on the head.

I'm sure the poor kid has no idea why I laugh every time I see him. I should probably tell him next Sunday.

Activity 5.11

Do people laugh when they see you? Assuming it's because you made them laugh first, what funny thing might you have said or done?

What amusing things can you remember from presentations you have attended? Without draining all the humor out of it, can you analyze the laughter-provoking incident and find a way to make it replicable?

Some humor, some connection with the audience or classroom of students can be planned ahead of time. Other connections come from being alert to opportunities as they arise. As the border patrol screener took the passport from the man in line ahead of me and then reached for mine, she asked, "Are you two together?" I smiled at the gentleman and replied, "Not yet."

Sometimes, as educators, we give it our best shot and the students or audience members don't seem to be getting it yet. But persistence and hope are essential components of our DNA. Similar to Annie Sullivan teaching the blind and deaf Helen Keller, we keep trying until we break through and the connection is made. Using the techniques recommended in this chapter will make it a lot easier to achieve those breakthroughs, those Helen Keller moments. So brace yourself. As a miracle worker, you can expect to see more smiles, more nodding heads, and a lot more standing ovations!

6

Harnessing humor

"If you're having fun, you're not learning."
—MATILDA, TriStar Pictures, 1996

So reads the banner above the blackboard in the classroom at Crunchem Hall Elementary School, where children are routinely terrorized by the principal, Miss Trunchbull. From her first day in class, gifted student Matilda Wormwood begins her own counter-terrorist pranks that eventually drive out the principal and restore the joy of fun-filled learning to the school.

Imagine that you are the sweet Miss Honey, Matilda's classroom teacher. You have a few traditionally tedious things that you have to convey to your students, including mind-numbingly boring paragraph construction and topic sentences. With the old banner gone, your goal is to bring tears of laughter to the eyes of your students. You start the lesson by saying: "I just heard this great new joke. Want to hear it?" Then you proceed to tell the joke with great enthusiasm, but with the lines all mixed up.[1] The punch line is somewhere in the middle and the last line isn't funny at all. At this point, you break out belly-laughing (excellent for *your* immune system) and look totally puzzled that your students don't get it. You repeat the last line (not funny) and you laugh some more. When you've giggled, chortled, and snorted for all you're worth, you flick on the LCD projector and display the mixed-up joke on the screen or interactive whiteboard as an editable document. Here's a colorful joke scramble from Michael Jursic, a teacher at Ryerson Community Public School in Toronto, Canada:

> The man says, "Great, and this will help my seasickness?"
>
> A man goes to the doctor. He says, "Doctor, I am going on a
>
> cruise for my honeymoon, and my problem is, I get seasick!"
>
> Just before you get on the ship, eat all this stuff whole, without
>
> chewing." The doctor says, "No, but it'll look really pretty
>
> in the water." Doctor says "No problem, just slice up
>
> one yellow pepper, one green pepper, and quarter 4 tomatoes."

You wait a few seconds to see if some bright student realizes that rearranging the sentences could vastly improve the joke. If the students are too busy worrying about your apparent lack of sanity, go ahead and move the first sentence and ask if that helps. Call for volunteers to move any remaining misplaced sentences.

Activity 6.1

Write and scramble a joke from three to five sentences in length.

If you are currently taking a class, submit your joke and the scrambled version to your teacher, professor, or the session presenter, who will select a few of the funniest ones to share (during the next class or after the break) with the rest of the group.

If you are currently teaching a class, try the joke scramble as a graded assignment (see the following rubric).

The joke could be assessed as follows:

Points	Category
0–10	Correct punctuation, grammar, spelling, and syntax; expressive and proper use of language
0–10	Positive humor (no off-color jokes; profanity; racial, ethnic, or sexist slurs; or otherwise putting people down)
0–10	Legible, attractive presentation and enthusiastic delivery

The grade would be calculated by multiplying the three scores above. (A perfect score or grade would be 1,000 points.) Any inappropriate language or negative humor would result in zero points for that second category and hence zero points for the total grade.

Besides this activity adding to your growing joke collection, students will have a good time and prove experientially the upgraded Crunchem Hall adage: "If you're having fun, you must be learning."

The beauty of an activity such as this is that students learn the *process* by laughing, doing, and laughing some more. Sequencing (now ingrained as fun!) can be used to organize myriad other content. A few possibilities are shown in the following table:[2]

Sections of short stories	*The Three Bears* and their chairs (lots of repetition for beginning or early language learners)
Stanzas of poems or songs	Especially lines that rhyme (popular songs are great motivators, or try imagist poems)
Steps in a recipe	This is especially fun if one person gives instructions for another to follow—literally.

Neoteny[1]

Before we continue, you ask, what exactly does humor look like in an educational setting? First of all, forget boring, hackneyed pedagogies and methodologies. What we need are neotenous[3] pranks—pranks full of youthful exuberance—that can lure students and audience members alike to tune in rather than drop (or walk) out. Yes, we want a resource bank of jokes, cartoons, funny images, and great one-liners. But, more important, we want to establish a kind of humor zone permeated with contagious playfulness. We want to reverse the current trend reported by Dr. Humor: "Preschool children laugh or smile on the average of over four hundred times per day, while adults over thirty-five only fifteen times per day."[4]

I can't say for sure whether it's a cause or just a coincidence, but the K–12 curriculum in the United States seems to parallel the decline in smiling. In fifth grade, we study Lewis and Clark and learn how one young woman named Sacagawea saved the entire expedition. By eighth grade we are studying the Great Depression, when people were throwing themselves out of windows because they had "lost everything" in the stock market.

Given a choice, it just seems like a lot more fun to work at the preschool or elementary-school level. I think of the young children I've worked with. My great-niece Taylor who (every morning when I have the privilege of staying next door at her grandma's place) greets me with a big grin and cheerful anticipation: "What are we going to play first, Auntie Nanelle?" She's the joy of my life. Lifts me to that four hundred range every time.

Or the students in my niece Shaila's second-grade class in Tigard, Oregon, who helped me create a weather report out of their spelling list. It rains 247 days a year there, so predicting rain was a no-brainer. But then we had it raining everything on the spelling list. Soon our weathercasters were sillier than Dr. Seuss. Laughing, high-fiving, pretending to duck under umbrellas and squealing "eeeuuu" every time something yucky fell from the sky.

Neoteny. It's all about keeping the childlike whimsy, the joy we had before we entered kindergarten—and sustaining it throughout our lives. Dr. Humor tells the story of his seventy-six-year-old mother whose oldest son finally worked up the nerve to ask her what kind of arrangements she wanted when "that day" finally came. Would she prefer cremation? What kind of service would she want? Without missing a beat, and with a perfectly straight face, she responded: "I don't know, honey. Surprise me."[5]

Surprise!

That's probably the next most important aspect of humor—surprise. The juxtaposition of the unexpected.[6] You think you are going down one path, and suddenly, at the last moment, it takes a detour. For example, students often take their own path on math problems:

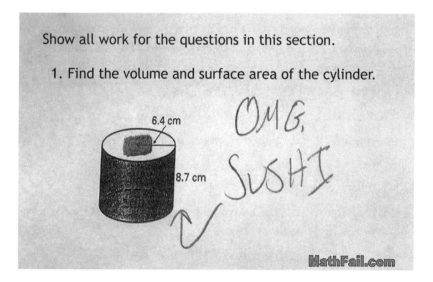

The brain is totally and repeatedly amused by these "detours." Like a dog chasing a Frisbee, it never seems to tire of making the leap.

Historical perspective

Neoteny (childlike exuberance), surprise (unexpected detours), and, what was the third part of my definition of humor? Oh, yeah: historical perspective (as in "someday you'll look back on this and laugh"). How many of our funniest stories are about events that were not so funny at the time?

Activity 6.2

Alone or with your class, brainstorm events that are funnier now than they were then. Try to find examples from a classroom or presentation experience. Did you learn a lesson from the incident?

Defining humor

For a clear, concise, and better-than-dictionary definition of humor, I turn to mirthologist Stephen Sultanoff, who identifies the following three components:

- Wit, the cognitive experience of "getting it"
- Mirth, the emotional experience of "feeling it"
- Laughter, the physiological experience[7] of "jiggling it"

Okay. I made up the "jiggling" part, but I think Dr. Sultanoff would approve.

Wit would, of course, include oxymorons—peace force, pretty ugly, only choice—and puns like such as

- Does the name Pavlov ring a bell?

- Dijon vu—the same mustard as before

- A lot of money is tainted. 'Tain't yours and 'tain't mine.

No one falls off his chair laughing at witticisms. They are more like an intellectual gym where the brain can flex its muscles for admiring fans, including the one in the mirror.

Is there a place for puns in education? Case in point: One of the few things I remember from fourth grade is that the capital of Arkansas is Little Rock. Why? Because at age nine I thought I was so clever giving my incredibly cute classmate Doug Middlestadt a hint—"There's a little rock in Arkansas"—when we were quizzing each other on the state capitals. As I said, no one fell off any chairs, but the information stuck because it was linked to a lame pun in my brain. I wonder if Doug remembers. I wonder if he's still cute.

Is there a place for puns in presentations? I would say that a groan from your students or audience members is better than no response at all. At least you have auditory confirmation that they are brain-flexing!

Mirth, as Mark Twain astutely realized, "is the great thing, the saving thing, after all. The minute it crops up, all our irritations and resentments slip away, and a sunny spirit takes their place."

"As we experience the emotional sensation of mirth, other feelings such as depression, anxiety, and anger are, at least temporarily, eliminated."[8] It's as if the beating of our hearts synched up to the most propitious metronome for peace and joy, growth and learning. When we speak of positive humor, we are generally referring to the good "vibes" generated and emanated by mirth.

Activity 6.3

Over the next ten days, keep a mirth journal in which you record eruptions of mirth that you observe, experience, and instigate. Note if and how the incidents change your mood and also if being more aware of mirth attracts more of it into your life. Prepare an example of mirth to share, emphasizing how it can create an atmosphere more conducive to stress-free teaching and learning.

Laughter is when the body gets actively involved with the humor. The abdomen jiggles and massages the internal organs. Tears of joy bathe the eyes and blood rushes to the face, warming and nourishing the skin. What does it cost? Every educator's favorite four-letter word: It's *"free!"* And kids come to school already knowing how to do it! Sometimes the adults need a little refresher but usually one hearty laugh is all it takes. And I have yet to receive a presentation evaluation saying: "You were *too* funny." Well, actually, I have, but I think that person meant it in a good way because she drew a big smiley face next to the comment.

When humor meets content

I am very serious about my content. And that is precisely why I have to make my audiences laugh. A lot. After a two-hour seminar, a woman came up to me crying, choking out the words: "I haven't laughed this hard in decades." (Must have been a district-office administrator.) Another woman thanked me profusely because she was convinced that the laughter had done more for her than her "last two years of chemotherapy." But my favorite comment came from a superintendent at an executive summit. He approached me at the morning break and said, "I was sure I wasn't learning anything because I was laughing so much. But then I realized . . ." and he proceeded to list for me every major point we had covered in the last ninety minutes.

Two things need to happen to get your content across:

- First, you have to get your audience's attention, that is, that annoying little interruption between naps. (As former-president Ronald Regan reportedly told his advisors: "Wake me up if something important happens anywhere in the world—even if I'm in a Cabinet meeting.") From my empirical research for over thirty years as an educator and presenter, no one has managed to laugh and fall asleep at the same time.

- Second, you need to connect the humor to your content. According to Peter Jonas, if you connect your point to humor, your students and your audiences remember it "32 percent better. Sixteen percent better even if the humor sucks."[9]

This is because of the way the brain thinks. As we've learned, the brain loves to make connections. It registers new input by connecting it to something that's already there. If it connects to something negative, we feel anxious and fear we do not have the resources to deal with it. If it connects to something positive, we embrace it and feel confident that we have the resources to enjoy it.[10]

This is where the advice to presenters to "start with a joke to warm up the audience" can miss the point. If the joke is unrelated to the presentation content, it's a waste of precious time and only gets the audience members' hopes up and makes them more disappointed if the rest of the presentation is boring. The worst example I saw of this was a workshop in which the presenter handed out little joke cards to every member of the audience. Every few minutes—it was set into her agenda like an alarm clock—she would call on someone to read his joke. The jokes were more random than funny and never had any connection to the material. It was as if she poked you to wake up but then gave you no reason why. I don't remember any of the jokes, much less any of the content.

Activity 6.4

Right now. Take three to five minutes. Stop whatever you are doing and make yourself laugh. Not the smirk of superiority that creeps over your face when you've come up with a good pun. Not even the gurgling giggle you enjoy over the whimsical antics of a silly child. No, what we need here is the full monty. If necessary, you can ease your way into it. Perhaps start by faking a guffaw, which should lead to chortles, which always degenerate into snorts and other loud expressions of amusement and, of course, the inevitable tears and convulsions.

Before you stop laughing, understand that you can use that energy to catapult serious content into long-term memory. Sure, your students, your audiences would be happy enough if you just made them laugh but remember that we are not the Comedy Club. We are responsible for making them remember our content as well.

Think back to the Super Bowl commercials from the year 2000. Do you remember the one when a bunch of cowboys was herding cats?[11] The advertisers took a common expression for something extremely difficult to do (herd cats) and made it into a hilarious video of cowboys whose faces were ripped to shreds but who "wouldn't do nothin' else." "It ain't an easy job, but when you bring a herd into town, and you ain't lost a one of 'em, there ain't a feelin' like it in the world." So entertaining that you'll never forget it. But who were the sponsors who paid to produce and air that ad? What was the product they wanted you to go out and purchase after the game?

There is one other risk with using humor. Sure, there's the research about how laughing out loud is healthy, healing, and even life-extending.[12] From Voltaire[13] to William F. Fry[14] and Norman Cousins[15] to Patch Adams[16]—everyone agrees that laughter is good medicine. In 2002, Lee Berk of Loma Linda University even ran an experiment that *quantified* the chemical changes:

- Increased endorphin levels by 27 percent (elevates mood)

- Increased human growth hormone by 87 percent (optimizes immunity)

- Decreased cortisol by 39 percent and adrenaline by 70 percent (lowers stress)[17]

But, as with all prescriptions, there are potentially dangerous side effects. As reported by "responsible healer" Hank Hyena:

- In 1989, Ole Bentzen was killed in a movie theater by John Cleese's antics in *A Fish Called Wanda*. The Dane's happy heart was destroyed when his pulse approached five hundred beats per minute.

- Sir Thomas Urquhart—translator of the ribald French author Rabelais—also died laughing in 1660 when he heard that the jovial libertine Charles II was ascending to the British throne.

- On January 30, 1962, three schoolgirls in the Kashasha village in present-day Tanzania started laughing and could not stop. Sent home, they transmitted their hysteria to the neighboring villages of Nshamba and Kanyangereka. The epidemic lasted six months. One thousand people were infected and fourteen schools were closed. Western psychologists categorize the plague as "Mass Psychogenic Illness" (MPI). Sadly, there is no record of the original joke. If discovered, it could provide a more economical and humane alternative to traditional warfare.[18]

Assuming you can steer clear of John Cleese, libertine British royals, and Tanzanian village girls, how safe do you feel about using humor in your presentations? Do you have the resources to pull it off? How do you become that teacher, that presenter whose name alone suffices to make people smile and whose content remains forever unforgettable?

You can spend an inordinate amount of time on the Internet searching for humorous images. Alternatively, for really funny pictures, germane to your content, you can put your own eye behind the lens. You know the hard points to teach and present. Whatever the subject, it goes down better with humor. Planning a presentation for a conference in Alaska? Teaching your fourth-grade students about our forty-ninth state? Open with a picture of this perfect place to stay (between Anchorage and Wasilla).

Need a laugh? Fly to the other end of the country and take a picture of the "Laugh" sculpture at the Botanical Gardens in Atlanta, Georgia. You have my permission to flash this image on the screen whenever you tell a groaner and your audience needs to be reminded of the healthful benefits of laughter.

If you're fortunate enough to be in the classroom, you have an additional twenty (or more) pairs of eyes on the world. Encourage your students to use their digital cameras and camera phones to conduct "humor journalism." Then sit back and enjoy some side-splitting world views.

Activity 6.5

Find two funny images: one that you have taken yourself and one that you find online (try typing *funny* into a search box). For the online image, select an image that is "labeled for reuse," in the public domain, or under the Creative Commons license (which makes the image available to the public for free and legal use, sharing, repurposing, and remixing).

If you are working in groups, present your images to the rest of the group and describe the context in which you might use each photo in the classroom or for a presentation.

I found this image, called "Dandelion," on Flickr.[19] The image made me think of situations when you could use balloons to increase static electricity and decrease stress at the same time. It would be great fun before a break in a presentation or before the group photo at the end of a workshop; a hoot before recess in a classroom; and just what the doctor ordered before a budget crisis meeting at the district office. All you need is a bag of balloons from the Dollar Store and this adorable photo as inspiration!

Several of the best-known image sites (for example, Google, Wikimedia, Flickr) also have video libraries. In addition, you will want to visit TeacherTube, SchoolTube, and YouTube and the budding collection at Next Vista for Learning.[20]

Activity 6.6

Investigate a site with online videos, choose a funny one, and describe the context in which you would use that video in the classroom or for a presentation.

Rather than downloading the video, you might post your work online with a link to the clip you are describing. Send me the link so I can laugh with you as I admire your work!

This is good stuff. Good and good for you. But is it enough? How many times have you attended a "really great" presentation by a Las

Vegas–caliber comedian (except with educational value and without dirty words) and by the time you left the room you couldn't remember any of the content and, hard as you tried, not even any of the jokes?

Yes, absolutely, we need to be funny as educators and educational presenters because we need to keep our students and our audiences awake. (Think of yourself as the bugler, playing reveille for the troops.) And sometimes, rarely, but we keep trying, with a really good humorous image, video clip, or story, we are able to connect that fun feeling to content that we want to hard-wire into long-term memory.

But, I would argue, the real value of humorous presentations is to create a humor zone in which the audience members and our students flex *their* humor muscles. When *they* instigate the humor and the laughter, it means that they have already made the connection. Their laughter comes out of *their* juxtaposition of new content with their prior knowledge.

We cannot have our schools (or our education-related presentations) be places of intimidation and discouragement, places where the banner over the door reads like the entrance to Dante's *Inferno*:

> Lasciate ogne speranza, voi ch'intrate.
> Abandon all hope, ye who enter here.[21]

We must create joyful spaces where everyone feels safe and encouraged to

> Laissez les bons temps rouler!
> Let the good times roll![22]

For example, imagine yourself in the classroom in Tacoma, Washington, where my brother, Wes Burmark, was teaching second grade. He was giving the little ones a spelling test, had already repeated several words and, frankly, was getting a bit cranky, when he got to "row." After still another student said "What?" Wes repeated "row, Row, ROW!" At that point, the entire class started singing "Row, row, row your boat." They finished the song and sat there grinning. That was twenty years ago. Wes still remembers it as if it were yesterday. I would wager that the kids do, too.

Speaking of singing, one of my most successful workshop activities was giving participants forty country-western song titles, including:

- "All My Exes Live in Texas"
- "Don't Believe My Heart Can Stand Another You"
- "I Got Through Everything but the Door"

Each group of three to six participants had to choose any twelve to fifteen of the titles and use those words to create a story in letter, poem, or narrative style. They could use partial titles and they could add up to twenty connector words. The final composition was to be between 100 and 125 words. Each small group had the opportunity to present its work.

The most memorable moment was when one strikingly attractive redhead was reading her group's story to the rest of the workshop attendees. She stopped dead in her tracks and blurted out: "All my exes *were* from Texas! All five of them!" The class howled. The connection was made to real life and, in her case, to prior knowledge and experience.

However that positive humor erupts from your students or your audiences, it's *their* laugh that makes knowledge stick. That big laugh, as Quincy Jones so powerfully puts it, that's "a really loud noise from the soul saying, 'Ain't that the truth.'"[23]

Amen.

7

Starting with images

Activity 7.1

Take a minute to look at this image and try to imagine the story behind the building it depicts. If you are in a class or workshop, divide into groups of three and take three minutes to discuss the photograph.

Have volunteers share with the large group what their small groups surmised.

What if you were in a high school English class studying Shakespeare's comedic play "The Taming of the Shrew"? This is clearly not 1594 or is it the oldest town in northern Italy. But could it be 1999? In *10 Things I Hate About You*, the teen movie riff on "The Taming of the Shrew," Padua High was a turreted brick edifice resembling a castle, perched atop a beautiful bay. Yes, this is the high school that provided the perfect backdrop for Patrick Verona (the late Heath Ledger) to pursue headstrong Kat Stratford (Julia Stiles). In fact, the school's football stadium is the setting for one of the film's most memorable scenes. During soccer practice, Patrick serenades Kat while dancing up and down the stone steps as he dodges the school's security police. (Check out Ledger's delightful performance in the YouTube video: "Can't Take My Eyes Off of You.")

The movie did not garner critical acclaim but the stadium scene is a hoot and could be an engaging way to lead teens into reading the Shakespearean play. Of course, it's all the more fun for students who currently attend the real Stadium High School (named after its bowl-shaped stadium) in Tacoma, Washington!

Now, for a different class, imagine that you are presenting the concept of "point of view." (This could be in a literature or writing class or in a situation when conflicting points of view are causing a problem and your presentation is charged with achieving consensus.) Instead of launching into some erudite and somniferous explanation of the abstract term, you project the following image as people enter the room:

Activity 7.2

Divide your class or audience into groups of three. Have each person pick one of the girls in the photo to role play. How is the focus of the birthday girl different from that of the girl sitting next to her or the girl sitting across from her?

Compile a list of the things that were similar and a list of the things that were different. Who was "right"?

From this activity, "point of view" has effectively defined itself.

Now say you are teaching World War II. Where do you start? One fun—and historically significant place—is with this iconic poster:

Activity 7.3

Take three to five minutes to look at this poster[1] and try to imagine the story of the woman it depicts. Note:

Three things you can observe

Two things you could infer

One question you would like to ask

If you have given your class this activity, at all cost resist the temptation to *name* the person in the poster. Once you do that, it's as if you have given the right answer, ending once and for all the need for any more interesting discussion or meaningful learning.

For the observations, keep soliciting contributions (and noting when the *observations* are really inferences—"Can you actually *see* that or do you just *suspect* from your experience that it's probably the case?") until there are no more different ones to be shared. If necessary, prompt with questions such as

- Is she wearing makeup?

- What is the position of the arms? The hands?

- What color is the bandana?

For the inferences—here's where you tap prior knowledge and its first-born child, prejudice—encourage all kinds of interpretations, again, until there are no more different ones to be shared. In case the class missed it, you might prompt with questions such as

- Why do you think she's wearing a bandana?

- What does the button on the shirt collar represent?

- Do you think she had collagen injections in those lips?

Again, resist the temptation to answer the questions on the spot. What seems like the fastest way to convey the information is actually the fastest way to stifle curiosity and halt the learning process. We all know that you know the answers. But if that were the goal, we could all have packed up and gone home a long time ago. No, the answers to those questions are the responsibility of your students and the attendees of your presentations!

Setting the stage

What you have just experienced in these three examples of starting with an image—Stadium High School, the birthday photo, and the World War II propaganda poster—embraces the conventions of live theater rather than the traditions of words and images on a printed page. We started with what the audience sees when the curtain rises.

When I was discussing terminology for stage sets with a friend who travels from event to event setting up technology support for live performances, his five-year-old granddaughter (my invaluable and oft-quoted consultant Emma) volunteered: "It's like the play I went to with my class last month. When they opened the curtains, you saw a bed with all the blankets and bedspread and pillows, so you knew right away you were in a bedroom."

"Right away." The actors and actresses do not come out onto a bare stage and say: "Imagine that I'm in my bedroom. [Verbal description.] Got that image? Okay, then, now I can deliver my first line." On the contrary: It's the job of the set designers to build and display a backdrop that lures the audience into the scene just in time for the action to begin.

Activity 7.4

Think about three potential stage sets for the play Emma's class attended:

1. Bare stage
2. Stage with PowerPoint screen and bullet points describing scene
3. Actual bedroom furniture

Which is the most efficient way of engaging the audience?

Think about these points when setting the stage for your next presentation:

- Are you wasting serious potential? Presentations consultant Olivia Mitchell[2] compares presenting on a bare stage (without visuals on your PowerPoint slides as a backdrop) to driving a Porsche at 50 kilometers (31 miles) per hour.

- How long is your presentation? Would it help to convey some background information more quickly? Research has demonstrated that humans process visuals sixty thousand times faster than text.[3] This is because images are processed *simultaneously* (like snapping a picture) and text is processed *sequentially* (think of keyboarding letter after letter after letter).[4]

What are some characteristics of a good stage set? A good backdrop for the actors' performance? When we go to the movies or attend a live performance, we tend to suspend our disbelief. After an initial gasp or two, we totally buy into the setting and don't give it any further *cognitive* attention. But in order to co-opt the magic, it helps to go behind the scenes and *think* about why the designers built the sets and chose the lighting that they did.

Activity 7.5

For this activity, think about the stage sets. To prime the cognitive pump, check out websites or YouTube for images and videos of performers you enjoy. Cirque du Soleil and *The Lion King* on Broadway might be good places to start. But also consider lower-budget performances such as a local church's Christmas program or a high-school musical. Or even a movie in which the scenery created a unique ambiance for the story to unfold.

Make a list of three or four things in the set or the scenery that contributed to your enjoyment of the performance(s). Pay particular attention to things you could replicate or adapt for your own presentations. If you are in a class, share your examples and your list with other members in your class or workshop.

Keep your list of characteristics of exemplary three-dimensional *stage sets*. Refer back to it as we discuss characteristics of exemplary one-dimensional *screen captures* for your slideshow presentations. The stronger the correlation, the better your slides!

Using images that illustrate

For our educational presentations, first and foremost, we want to keep the visual elements on our slides illustrative. As Cliff Atkinson shares in *Beyond Bullet Points*, "Research has found that visuals can improve learning, but only if they illustrate the point you are making, . . . if they tell a major part of the story as they communicate information through the visual channel in synch with your verbal explanation, but not when pictures are added for decorative effect."[5]

For example, the title slide of my presentation, "Making Education Stick: Veni, Vidi, Velcro (I Came, I Saw, It Stuck)," has the perfect opening image:

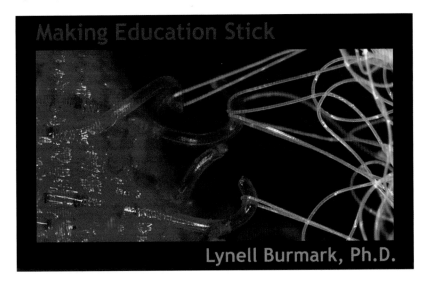

The magnified Velcro image[6] is the anchor, the backdrop for the entire presentation.

Activity 7.6

By yourself or with a partner go through title slides of your presentations or peruse those posted on www.slideshare.net or other hosting sites for freely shared presentations.

Using the illustrative criterion, find one exemplary or one particularly bad opening slide. Remember, we are not looking for an ugly slide but rather a slide whose image does not illustrate the topic at hand. Share your find and critique at your next class meeting or training session or post them to a designated site where everyone can access them.

Make sure you use examples that do not violate any copyrights and, as always, cite your source.

In most instances, the title slide is displayed for a longer time than any other slide in your presentation. It is also the first impression you make—what the audience sees when the curtain rises. If you repeat that same image on your closing slide, you have a second chance to firmly hook it (along with all the content you "stick" to it) into the long-term memory of your audience.

Focusing on the essentials

A second criterion for the visual content of our slides is to distill its essential elements. As educators, we have learned to be realistic about what can be covered in a class period. We need to establish similar limits for our presentations. As writer Tom Johnson puts it, let's not try to cover *Moby Dick, War and Peace,* and *Les Misérables* when we only have time for Dr. Seuss's *One Fish, Two Fish, Red Fish, Blue Fish.*[7]

Within the presentation, we must also learn to limit what we put on each individual slide. It's a boardroom legend and an education myth that people learn more if you can cram more onto your slides. The truth is that people learn better when extraneous information is removed.[8]

The master of this concept is Nancy Duarte. Chapter Eleven in her *slide:ology* book, "Interacting with Slides," contains this wonderful segment on "Reducing Text on a Slide."[9] The purpose of the slide is to support the presenter's explanation of learning to ride a bicycle using training wheels. It is the best procedure I've seen anywhere on weaning presenters from using their slides as teleprompters:

Step one: Select a slide that has too many words on it.

> # Learning to Ride
> - **Put training wheels on the bike**
> - **Raise the training wheels so you wobble**
> - **Wear clothing and a helmet to protect yourself**
> - **Remove the training wheels and practice falling on the grass**
> - **Enjoy riding your bike wherever you need to go**

Step two: Highlight one key word or short phrase per bullet and rehearse the slide until you can remember all the content when you look only at the highlighted word.

> # Learning to Ride
> - **Put training wheels on the bike**
> - **Raise the training wheels so you wobble**
> - **Wear clothing and a helmet to protect yourself**
> - **Remove the training wheels and practice falling on the grass**
> - **Enjoy riding your bike wherever you need to go**

Step three: Remove all other text on the slide, leaving just the key words as mnemonics.

Learning to Ride

- Training wheels
- Wobble
- Clothing
- Grass
- Go!

Step four: Add an image!

Learning to ride

- Training wheels
- Wobble
- Clothing
- Grass
- Go!

Can you see how this four-step process could move your presentations towards image-filled, text-free slides? Eventually, you would actually *start* with the image and not ever put any text on the slide (except, perhaps, in the speaker's Notes View). But, for now, you may want to use the four-step process as your training wheels.

Activity 7.7

Find a text-only slide in one of your presentations and take it through the four-step process. If you are in a class, share your process (and result) at your next class meeting or training session or post your work to a designated site where everyone can access it.

Sizing and placing images

Once you have found a compelling, appropriate, illustrative image, and reduced the content on the slide to its essential elements (in most cases, a single image), you can focus on the purposeful placement of that image on the slide.

You may have noticed that the training wheels image (and the "You Can Do It!" poster) did not fill the 1,280-pixel width of my standard-sized illustrations. In both cases, I did not have a choice (the training wheels image came from the *slide:ology* book and the poster by its very essence is shaped like a poster).

True confessions? Before I knew better, I used to create title slides in which smallish images were symmetrically and boringly balanced with the presentation title and my name.

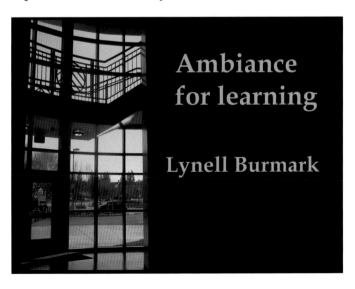

But now I avoid using images that don't fill the slide. Think of our stage-set metaphor. When the curtains open, how would it look if the "set" filled one-third or one-half of the stage and the rest of the space was some kind of blank wall? How would that affect your ability to suspend disbelief in order to feel, to believe, that you had actually entered that place?

Particularly annoying are those images that *almost* fill the screen. More true confessions? I, too, have committed the almost-filled-screen transgression. Yes, sadly, it happened on more than one occasion during that painful transition period moving from XGA (old TV-shaped images) to WXGA (more like the wider, HDTV-shaped images). My friend Lou suggested just stretching my images to fit.

Turns out that Lou wasn't any happier than the rest of my friends to appear 25-percent wider in all my slides.

So, I turned to another friend—Photoshop—for professional assistance. (*Note:* If you are *not* a geek, copy these four steps, send them to your favorite tech-user, and move on to the next paragraph.)

In Photoshop,

1. Choose *File... Open* and select the XGA image you want to resize.

2. Go to *Image... Canvas Size* and set the width and height to *pixels.* (Width will be 1,024 and height will be 768.)

3. Crop the height to 640 pixels using the anchor to designate whether you want the image cropped top, bottom, or both.

4. Go to *Image... Image Size... Document Size.* From the pull-down menu select *percent* and—in either the *Width* or *Height* box— type in 125 (percent). (Your new width will be 1,280; new height will be 800.)

This will work for 80 percent of your images.

For the other 20 percent (where faces had their chins cut off and brains were lobotomized), you may have to resort to more drastic (and time-consuming) measures such as the tedious cloning of backgrounds out to the sides or finding a different image in the wide-screen-aspect ratio.

Moving forward, the key when taking photographs is to think wide screen; the tip to finding right-sized images on Google is to go to *Advanced search* and pull down the *aspect ratio* of *wide*. We need images that will completely fill a WXGA screen with what graphic artists refer to as a "full bleed." According to presentation designer Garr Reynolds, "Full-bleed images offer ultimate impact."[10] Instead of inserting an image in a frame or box on a portion of the screen and then putting the text on the remaining background space, fill the screen with a "full-bleed" image so that the entire background is covered. "Now the image becomes the background and the type becomes part of the image, creating a more dynamic, engaging visual."[11]

How can you get a high-quality image with specific parts of the photo left blank enough for words? Reynolds shares how business professionals do it: iStockphoto's CopySpace. Just create a free account at iStockphoto, then go to *Advanced search*.[12] In *Search with CopySpace*, click squares in the three-by-three (nine-square) grid to specify areas of the photo to remain blank. Enter a keyword and cancel your appointments for the rest of the day.

If you have zero budget for buying stock photos (in other words, if you are an educator), remember that you have at least twenty to thirty photographers working for you for free. (They're called students.) Show them the grid and have them be on the lookout for great shots. And, of course, have them help you sort through photographs on free image sites such as www.imageafter.com.

That's where I found this great backdrop for the Norman Vincent Peale quote I use in the *Emotions* segment of my "Making Education Stick" workshops.

"Throw your heart over the fence and the rest will follow."

—Norman Vincent Peale

As Garr Reynolds suggests in his earlier work, *Presentation Zen*, "a simple quote is a good springboard from which you can launch your next topic or . . . support your point. The trick is not to use them too much and to make sure that they are short and legible."[13]

Activity 7.8

Find a quotation that you could use in an upcoming lesson or presentation and place it over a photograph that you have taken or a copyright-free image from the Internet.

If you are in a class, arrange to share your slide.

So, in placing our images on the screen, we have moved from visuals that fill a relatively small portion of the screen to annoying ones that *almost* fill the screen to full-bleeds. Is that the limit? What do you think?

Activity 7.9

Take a moment to reflect. How could you make the image bigger than the screen?

Let's look at two techniques for taking the image beyond the edge of the screen.

First, as Garr Reynolds describes it, there is the option of building visual interest by "hiding" part of an object "offstage."[14] He describes a performance by the Cirque du Soleil in which sounds were generated offstage and the dancers moved back and forth from the stage into the audience—all making the stage feel much larger than it really was. He contends that we can do something similar with our presentation slides. We can use the "implied space" beyond what the viewer can see on the screen to create "an interesting visual tension. Implied space also takes advantage of the closure principle, our natural tendency to complete or close images."[15]

A great photographic example is this shot of the Red Bull International Air Race in which the plane's condensation trail (contrail) continues off behind the plane into the sky.

Photo by Nuno Gomes

Activity 7.10

Keep an eye out for images in print advertisements that bleed into the "implied space" off the edge of the advertisement. Particularly when the image implies motion—for example, a fast car driving off the right-hand edge or a bottle of wine peeking in from the left-hand edge to pour its ruby red contents into a welcoming goblet—this treatment can add to the "experience." Also watch for billboards and presentation slides that use this technique well. Be thinking about a concept you need to communicate that could use some over-the-top, off-the-edge visual tension. Try it. It will have an impact.

Another interesting technique to extend the image comes from the San Francisco De Young Museum's annual floral fine art exhibit, "Bouquets to Art," which juxtaposes floral displays with the works that inspired them.[16]

What role did the selection of colors have in the pairings? What is lost in the grayscale mode?

Color!

In so many ways, color is how we identify our world. It's how we spot the fruit on the tree.

And how we realize the season's changed.

It's quick to grab attention.[17]

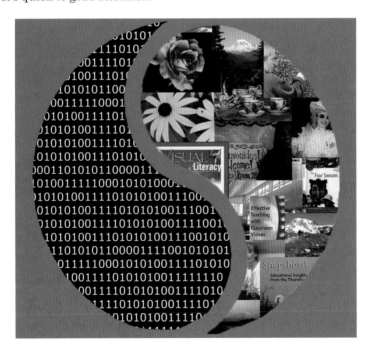

And show us where to stare.[18]

To organize our classroom stuff.

And display which their is there.[19]

there • their • they're

Once upon a time, there were three little pigs. There was Curly. He was the oldest. There was Wurly. He was the smartest. And then there was Flo. She was the favorite pig. Their mother loved Flo the best.

One day, when the boys stole Flo's allowance, Mama sent them to live with their uncle, Oscar Mayer. Uncle Oscar always knew what to do with bad little pigs.

Flo and Mama Pig still live in their high-rise in New York City and they're very happy there. Now Flo gets her brothers' allowance because they're not there any more.

Gina Corsun
Herbert Hoover Middle School
Edison, New Jersey

Today's students did not grow up with *Leave It to Beaver* and *The Andy Griffith Show,* so it's not surprising that a group of high-school students complained about the black-and-white Mathew Brady photographs[20] their teacher was using to illustrate lessons on the Civil War.

One student asked the teacher why he didn't use the color versions? Another student volunteered: "Maybe people were that color back then." Apparently it's difficult to take a historical perspective when you were born thirty years after color television replaced black and white.

The important points to remember when preparing presentations are that

- Color visuals increase willingness to read by up to 80 percent.

- Using color can increase motivation and participation by up to 80 percent.

- Color enhances learning and improves retention by more than 75 percent.[21]

Even one highlight color can make a huge difference.

Activity 7.11

Try this with students or other audience members. Pick three words of similar length (shorter words for young children, longer words for adults). Display them on a dark gray background with two of the words in very light gray and one word in a bright red. Give the audience members three to five seconds to look at the words. Then cover the words and test to determine which ones the audience can remember. Compare the percentage that remembered the word in red versus the percentage that remembered the other two words.

Did you ever wonder why—in mostly black-and-white advertisements—the designers put one element (usually the name of the product or the company's toll-free phone number) in bright red? The time it takes to locate a target word within a document is improved up to 74 percent if that word is in color.[22]

Again, for educators, it's less about the aesthetics than about what affects learning. Purposeful use of color can attract attention and improve retention. What else can you do (and at no extra cost in the digital world) that has so much impact?

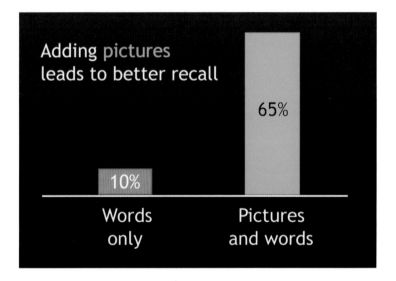

If information is presented orally, people remember about 10 percent, tested seventy-two hours after exposure. That figure goes up to 65 percent if you add a picture.[23]

Of everything in the human sensory toolbox, states John Medina, "vision is probably the best single tool we have for learning anything.... The more visual the input becomes, the more likely it is to be recognized—and recalled. The phenomenon is so pervasive, it has been given its own name: the pictorial superiority effect, or PSE."[24]

Human PSE is truly Olympian. Tests performed years ago showed that people could remember more than 2,500 pictures with at least 90 percent accuracy several days postexposure, even though subjects saw each picture for about ten seconds. Accuracy rates a year later still hovered around 63 percent. In one paper—adorably titled "Remember Dick and Jane?"[25]—picture recognition information was reliably retrieved several decades later.[26]

Combining words and images

So do we need words at all, especially in this treatise on images? Wouldn't giving you a digital photo album to click through be a faster, more efficient way to Velcro my information to your brain neurons?

Activity 7.12

Take a good look at the following photograph. What is the event? Who are these two people? What is their relationship? Why are they smiling? If you are in a class, break out into small groups to discuss and then share in the large group until all different opinions have been expressed.

We'll come back to the story behind this photograph later. For now, let me just say that when I do this activity with live audiences, they recognize me as the petite blonde in the red coat. Speculations run the gamut on the handsome gentleman standing beside me. Audience members mine their own life experiences to come up with an explanation, thereby giving credence to the words of French author Anaïs Nin: "We don't see things as they are. We see them as we are."[27]

For you to see what I see, to know what really happened on that sunny October day in northern California, you need *two* input tracks:

1. The colorful visual big picture in the photograph

2. The audio of my colorful overlay narration of the details of the actual event

The best of both worlds—audio and visual—join together in synergistic harmony. Of course, we revel in these unions day in and day out without even consciously thinking about it. But Allan Paivio, emeritus professor of psychology at the University of Western Ontario, has spent decades researching the phenomenon that he refers to as *dual-coding*. His theory "postulates that visual and verbal information are encoded and decoded by separate, specialized perceptual and cognitive channels in the brain.[28]

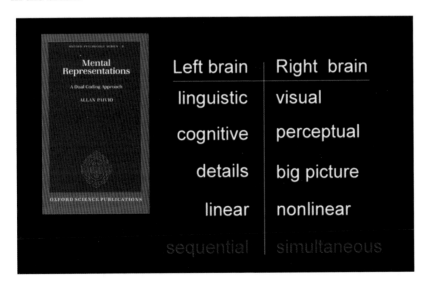

Left brain	Right brain
linguistic	visual
cognitive	perceptual
details	big picture
linear	nonlinear
sequential	simultaneous

In "Teaching Visual Literacy in a Multimedia Age," Glenda Rakes offers more evidence to support Paivio's dual coding theory:

> Using positron emission tomography (PET scans), medical researchers have been able to demonstrate that different areas of the brain become active when individuals are exposed to verbal and visual information. When individuals were asked to look at and remember verbal information, two regions in the brain's verbal domain—the left hemisphere—became active. When presented with visual information, the right hemisphere lit up.
>
> Given this information, the use of visuals in instructional materials takes on a larger dimension than when simply thought of as decorative supplements to text. The use of visuals with text can provide that dual code that can, in turn, increase comprehension.[29]

This is complemented by Richard Mayer's research that claims retention and recall are boosted 42 percent and transfer a whopping 89 percent with illustrated texts![30]

When we mix images and text, the eye will go to the images first, then the text (which viewers will process visually, pixel by pixel, tediously translating little dots into letters, letters into words, words into phrases and, we hope eventually, phrases into meaning). As any reading teacher can verify, the speed of that translation process will vary. But no matter the reading rate, almost everyone can read words faster than he can say them out loud. (If you doubt this, pick a paragraph and time yourself.) Consequently, in a live presentation, when speakers read the text from their slides, audience members reading those same bullet points will rarely be in synch with each other and virtually never in synch with the speaker.

How much of a problem is this? Imagine a video or movie in which the synchronized sound track is ahead or lagging by a few seconds. Jarring? Distracting? Annoying? How long would you put up with that before just turning off the video or walking out of the theater?

Is there a better way? Is it possible to avoid that hopeless task of trying to synch up our words with the wildly differing reading speeds of our students and audience members? In a word, *yes*! In five words: *no text on the screen.* With no on-screen text, words are forced into the audio channel that we can synchronize *on the fly* with the images on our screens.

Of course, the best way to be insanely great on the fly is, ironically, to do intensely purposeful preparation. First, we do the serious work of gathering all those compelling images for the presentation. And then, during the presentation, we remember to carry out one easy—but easy-to-forget—presentation strategy: to *time-delay* the delivery of the narration that we voice-over our slides.

When we use still images, or *stills,* we can delay the onset of the "audio track" just long enough—from an almost imperceptible one to two seconds to up to twenty seconds if there is a lot to contemplate in the "visual track"—to give our students or audience members the opportunity to connect what they see to relevant prior knowledge in order to prepare themselves for what they will hear next. See and hear. Show and tell. Always follow that sequence.

Now take a few seconds to look again at the image I shared earlier.

Do the lanyards and badges awaken memories of an event you have attended in the past? Do the smiles remind you of a wonderful relationship you have rekindled? Would you like to know what *really* happened?

Last October I went to my Stanford University reunion. One of the "Classes Without Quizzes" was a "Hilarity Workshop" by popular Stanford professor emeritus Jack Bunzel. I arrived early to make sure to get a good seat. (A "good seat" is, by my definition, next to an attractive male not sitting next to an attractive female.) I began chatting with the gentleman in the good seat next to mine and when he seemed genuinely interested in what I did for a living I handed him my business card. He gasped and said: "No, it can't be! Mademoiselle Burmark? You were my French teacher here at Stanford! I'm still taking French because of you!" Then, he added, shyly: "You probably didn't notice that I had a crush on you." I'm looking at him, thinking: "Why didn't you *say* something?" Anyway, to make a long story short, this picture was taken the next morning. By his wife. Nice woman who concurred: "So, *you're* the French teacher. He talks about you all the time."

I share this picture and this story with you for two reasons:

First, to remind you (and me, too) that as educators we do make a difference. How many students are out there whom we don't even know about who are taking French or teaching school or serving others in an amazing capacity because of some spark that we ignited in them? How blessed are we to be able to pay our passion forward?

And second, as wonderful as our photographs may be, without our words, our impassioned overlay narration, they will never hang in the gallery that our students and audience members are constructing to add beauty and meaning to their lives.

To illustrate the point of images plus narration, one of my favorite easy-to-replicate activities is the "Rapid Fire." Ideally, we would use three projectors with three huge screens, side by side by side. If your classroom or training venue is not that well equipped, consider using a triptych template that builds three images on one wide screen. How does Rapid Fire work? Instead of standing in front of an audience (or a classroom of students or your peers) and reading a report, you click through a slideshow of images that you narrate in one (rapid) minute.

In my example, I ask: "How many of you have been to India?" (Usually one or two hands will go up and those folks have traveled to Delhi or Mumbai.)

Well, today, class, I'm going to take you on a one-minute tour to the south of India, to the state of Kerala . . . . (Click, click, click, the images build on the screen.)

What image did you have in your mind's eye when I said *India*? Did you see this warm, sandy beach? (Click.)

Here's another image (click) I downloaded from the Internet—from the Kerala State Tourism Bureau of that same Varkala Beach. (Click.) And a photograph depicting the main industry in the region: fishing. The men go out every morning in their fishing boats and cast their nets. Fishing is a very lucrative industry in the area.

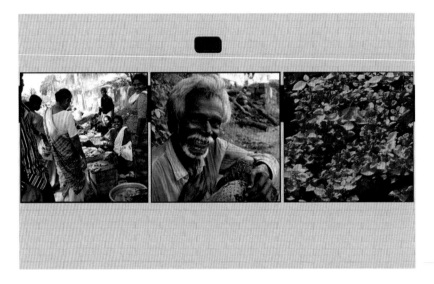

(Click.) Here you see the women in their beautiful silk saris buying that delicious fresh fish in the marketplace. Fish is the main staple of their diet. They cook it in spiced coconut milk . . . similar to Thai food. How many of you have had Thai food? Mmm. Yummy. (Click.) Here's a beggar in the marketplace. Not everyone is wealthy in Kerala, although the fishermen do quite well. (Click.) There is also a lucrative tourist business. The sun is always in the sky in this tropical climate that welcomes tourists to Kerala all twelve months of the year! Every way you turn there are colorful, tropical flowers.

(Click.) And swaying coconut palms.

(Click.) By the way, Kerala means "land of coconuts." Thanks for coming with me to Kerala, and (click) Varkala Beach![31]

Activity 7.13

After the one-minute trip to India, please answer the following questions:

1. What is the main industry in this area of India?
2. What is the staple food of the local people's diet?
3. How is it cooked?
4. What is another industry?
5. What time of year is the tourist season?
6. What does *Kerala* mean?
7. Would you like to visit Varkala Beach?

How tough was that test?

How would that little quiz compare to a test on the same material if I had read you the report with no pictures? Or had you read about it in a book with no illustrations?

How much do you think students would learn if they transformed their traditional reports into one-minute illustration and narration Rapid Fires? How much (more) would their classmates learn and remember from the reports? What would *your* Rapid Fire of this chapter look like?

Images *and* words—the synergy is irrefutable. And the payoff is life long.

8

Playing music

You have them for less than an hour. You want to make it an experience they'll never forget. You need to connect with them right away and break down any resistance to your message so your content can flow straight into their long-term memory.

Want a sure-fire plan with a "money-back" guarantee?

Ready? Two words: (1) Monet. (2) Bach. (No extra charge for bad puns.)

Really. It's that simple:

1. Images
2. Music

To lure us into their fantasy worlds, to complement their world-class images, successful media productions all use music. Think of classic television programs: *MASH. Cheers. Friends.* Can you hear the theme songs in your mind's ear? What about blockbuster movies: *Lawrence of Arabia*, *Titanic*, and *Slumdog Millionaire*? Who can forget "Lara's Song," "My Heart Will Go On," and "Jai Ho"?

Even before the "talkies" (movies with sound), producers and directors understood the need for music. During the era of the silent films (1891–1929), actors such as Charlie Chaplin and Buster Keaton had audiences on the edge of their seats, totally enraptured by their adventures, totally empathetic with their struggles of the heart.[1] How? In every one of the theaters—there was a pipe organ! Why the added expense for the organ and the organist? As University of California, Irvine research professor Norman Weinberger explains: The audience needed the music "to engage its [appropriate] emotional reactions and involvement."[2]

In today's movies, we get dialogue and amazing, bigger-than-life sound effects delivered in Dolby surround sound. And we still have music. Not a lone, melodramatic pipe organ, but everything from dueling banjos (*Deliverance*) to the full-blown orchestras that accompany most films today. Why do the movies still need music? According to Weinberger, "to supply the actual emotional states and feelings [the audience needs] to identify with [the action] and the characters involved."[3]

I would draw an analogy to the laugh track that overlays most television sit-coms (situation comedies). Whenever viewers hear that contagious burst of group laughter, they get a confirmation of their emotions—yes, this is funny, and yes, you are reacting appropriately by laughing at this point.

Of course, music is much more powerful and broadly applicable than a laugh track. It not only tells us when to laugh but also when to cry, get excited, relax, and so on. And although sometimes the laugh track can be annoying—and, rarely, even provoke dissent ("Come on, that wasn't even funny!")—a well-done music track weaves its magic on a more subliminal level and almost never elicits a push-back response. In fact, unless we are paying specific attention to the music (as the dramatic actors will do in Activity 8.1), we are not even consciously aware that the music is dictating our emotional state.

Activity 8.1

Invite three or four students or audience members to dramatize someone entering the room to begin a lesson, presentation, or ceremony. Queue up a different music clip for each grand entrance. *Note:* Each minidrama ends with the music fading and the "actor" delivering his or her first line. For the music clips, you can have students or participants provide their own (in multiple-session classes or workshops) or you can access the "Grand Entrance Clips" from the music folder on the DVD that accompanies this book.[4]

Another fun clip to use (or perhaps show as an example when making the assignment) would be the opening credits from the movie *Saturday Night Fever*, when a sexy, young John Travolta struts his stuff to the Bee Gees' "Stayin' Alive" lyrics: "Well, you can tell by the way I use my walk, I'm a woman's man: no time to talk . . ."

Whichever music selections you decide to use, afterward, in small groups, discuss how the music made you feel, how it put you in the mood for what was immediately to follow.

On that note, may I share one of my fantasies with you? All my life I've wanted to have my own theme song. Oh, yes. Whenever I entered the room, my particular song would announce my arrival. And that song would become so associated with me that whenever people heard it—even if I weren't present—they would think of me and remember something they had learned from me and smile.

Are you smiling? (Queue up the smile track.)

Activity 8.2

If you had to pick one well-known song to represent you, what would it be and why? Does that song somehow represent your essence? Does it lift your spirits and convey your hopes and dreams? If you feel comfortable doing so, share your song with others in the group.

I tease Bonnie St. John[5] that her song should be "Here Comes the Sun." She has a smile that lights up the room and her against-all-odds life story has inspired millions of people to make the most of their own lives.

My song could be "You Raise Me Up" as sung by Celtic Woman.[6] My desire to help *you* be the best you can be is definitely a driving force. But so far (as long as movie-star-level fame keeps eluding me), my presentations are not about me. This fact was brought home to me in a recent airport encounter when a woman rushed up to me shaking a pointed finger and announcing excitedly: "You! You! I can't remember your name but I've been using yellow letters on a blue background ever since I heard your presentation at the ASCD conference three years ago!" So, my music continues to accompany the presentation *content*, rather than the presenter *persona*. For example, to begin a recent presentation titled "Ambiance for Learning," I put images of sunflowers to the cheerful, original composition by Lou Marzeles's "Enlighten Up!"[7]

The musical slideshow prepared my audience to hear about the importance of bringing more natural sunlight into our classrooms—a major theme of architects who are transforming our schools from rows of prison cells into clusters of transparent learning studios.

Beloved storyteller and renowned digital storytelling coach Jason Ohler warns us about music taking over our emotions: "Like it or not, sappy music tends to make us feel sentimental (even if we don't want to), while the *Rocky* theme makes us feel powerful and conquering (even if we aren't). The *Jaws* theme can make *Bambi* appear evil. That's the power of music. Use it wisely."[8] His concern for student producers is that they rely too heavily on the music and fail to develop good digital stories. He asks: "Does the music drive the story, or is it the other way around? If the music were removed, how would the story fare?"[9]

If the music were removed . . .

If you haven't already been on the California Adventure ride "Soarin' over California" at Disneyland in Anaheim, California, or Disney World in Orlando, Florida, pause right now to put that on your bucket list. The ride is nothing short of amazing! For now, a low-resolution rendition can be found on YouTube.

Activity 8.3

Take four minutes and forty seconds and strap yourself in for a simulated hang glider tour of the Golden State.

Join eighty-six other passengers as you fly over the breathtaking Golden Gate Bridge in San Francisco, north to the redwood forests and the wine country, south and east to Monterey Bay, Lake Tahoe, Yosemite National Park, and culminating at Disneyland itself, where dusk turns to dark just in time for fireworks to light up the nighttime sky. Let the magnificent original music by film composer Jerry Goldsmith permeate every cell of your being.

(On the actual ride you are also treated to well-timed aromatic air streams, for example, orange blossoms for citrus orchards, evergreen needles for mountain scenes, and salt-water breezes for Monterey Bay. And you sway in the cantilevered, dangling seats whose subtle movements are synchronized to the film as it's projected on the large, concave movie screen that envelopes you throughout the flight.)

Music composer Jerry Goldsmith reputedly came out of his preview of the ride in tears, saying that he would gladly have written the music for free just to be part of something so exquisitely beautiful.[10]

Now—with apologies to Jerry—please replay the video *without the music*. Just the first thirty seconds or so. How is the experience different? Why?

To answer that, let's rewind the film a bit.

In the real world, sensations self-synchronize without any conscious effort on our part. When we see a bird, we hear it sing. When we see the sun, we feel its warmth on our cheek. When we see an orange, we smell its unique citrus fragrance. In the reel world—and most certainly while "Soarin' over California"—the synchronization of those separate sensual tracks is orchestrated for us. So, exactly how does the music fit in?

In the real world of our everyday experience we have an emotional as well as a sensual reaction to events. The experience may be colored by which side of the bed we rolled out of that morning or what nice (or nasty) remark someone just made to us. We have the freedom to choose our emotional attitude in any given set of circumstances.[11]

However, in the reel world, when we are watching *Titanic* or *Avatar*, for example, it's producer-director James Cameron who dictates our emotions. As audience members, when we agree to suspend our disbelief, if only for ninety minutes, to fully engage with the story, we also agree, albeit on a subconscious level, to suspend, to relinquish control of our emotions.

In order to make the reel real, *our* emotions need to be orchestrated along with all the other tracks put together for the film. The most efficient and effective way to do that? Use the music.

I must confess that I am sitting here literally trembling at the thought of that much power. Does it matter what music we (and our children!) listen to in any context, not just scored for the movies? And the music we play in our classrooms or during our presentations, do those selections make a difference? Isn't it just a question of musical taste? Or is there more to it?

To cite one of many research studies on this topic, at Cornell University Carol Krumhansl found that not only could listeners easily identify musical compositions as *happy, fearful,* or *sad,* but they also consistently exhibited the same physiological responses to the music as if they were physically experiencing those emotions: *happy* music led to the largest changes in respiration; *fearful* music to maximal changes in the rate of blood flow; and *sad* music the greatest changes in skin temperature, blood pressure, and heart rate. Alas, sad music can literally break your heart.[12]

So, the answer to "What music should we play in the classroom?" really has nothing to do with taste and everything to do with the physiological and emotional impact that music will have on listeners.

Activity 8.4

Consider grunge rock. Would you predict that it would increase or decrease listeners' feelings of the following emotions? Shade in the appropriate boxes. Do you see a pattern?

Grunge Emotions	Increase	Decrease
Caring		
Mental clarity		
Relaxation		
Vigor		
Hostility		
Fatigue		
Sadness		
Tension		

Compare your predictions with the results from a study conducted by the Institute of HeartMath.[13] After fifteen minutes of listening to grunge rock, the first four (positive) emotions were significantly decreased; the second four (negative) emotions were significantly increased.

This contrasted sharply with the impact of the more classical *Speed of Balance* composition specifically written and performed to facilitate mental and emotional balance:

Emotions on *Balance*	Increase	Decrease
Caring	✓	
Mental clarity	✓	
Relaxation	✓	
Vigor	✓	
Hostility		✓
Fatigue		✓
Sadness		✓
Tension		✓

Again, which kind of music do you want to put into your body? Into the bodies of your students? Your audiences?

Speaking of audiences, a few years back at the annual ASCD conference, I was scheduled to speak on stress reduction. As I recall, the presentation title was "Calm Before the Storm." Even though it was the last session on the last day of the conference, the room was packed. People were sitting in the aisle and even behind me on the stage; others were standing along the back and at least another twenty people were wedged in the double-doorway. I remember one belligerent attendee challenging me: "This better be good. I stayed for this!"

How could I respond to that? You've heard me say, "Don't spend forty-five minutes describing an okapi when you can spend four to five seconds displaying one on your LCD projector." (Start with the picture.) Well, this was a group that no picture—even putting that okapi on a beach in Maui with gently swaying palm trees in the background—would have done any good. I knew intuitively that music and humor were the only antidotes for that level of stress. The tension was so intense—and there was always the risk that my jokes would bomb—that I decided I'd better start with music. Besides, with music, there's no waiting for the punch line. Its effect starts with the first note you play.

Have you ever sung a lullaby to a baby and then felt it fall asleep in your arms? Is there anything on earth any sweeter than that? Well, yes. That stressed-out room full of administrators in Boston watching and listening to a music video.[14] Within seconds, all tension and hostility melted into total calm. Was I manipulating their emotions with music? Yes. Had they given me permission to do so? Most definitely.

Of course, the curse of being a teacher (born, raised, trained, deployed) is that I can't resist a teachable moment. Facing that crowd of sweetly smiling, blissed-out but still (mostly) conscious educators, I had to ask, albeit in dulcimer tones so as not to break the spell: "Can you feel the atmosphere in the room? Would you like me to play that again? Put it on continuous loop?" And, of course, I had to gently wave the handout in the air to remind them they had the information about ordering the video to use with their own students and professional development audiences.

So, how can *you* make the point about mood-altering music with *your* audiences—as you not only lift their mood but also teach them to lift the moods of the people they reach and teach? The simple juxtaposition of "Ain't No Sunshine When She's Gone" (Bill Withers) with "Sunshine on My Shoulders" (John Denver) would probably suffice. (End with John Denver. You don't want people *leaving* your session in a depressed state. Bad enough that they came in that way.) Or you could involve them in a little more theatrical activity:

Activity 8.5

Locate the instrumental piece "Moody Medley" in the music folder on the DVD that accompanies this book.[15]

Then, in your classroom or workshop, invite five to nine volunteers—depending on room size—to dramatize how the changes in music alter their moods. (The rest of the class or audience can stand up and "dance" along.)

When the music has finished playing, discuss how quickly music can change your mood. Talk about how to use music responsibly.

The key as an educator or presenter is to select music *intentionally.* You don't impose gratuitous music the way some PowerPoint presenters slap on dorky clipart. You select that perfect piece of music with as much loving care as you select the perfect anchor image (or video clip) to set the stage for the lesson or presentation to follow.

Do be prepared for a little readjustment from time to time. For example, my Pilates instructor, Debbie Honeycutt, usually does a wonderful job of putting on relaxing music so we can inhale pure joy and exhale all toxic thoughts as we tone up our abs and become the best conditioned females we can possibly be.

But, as I had to explain to her last week, "There's a fine line between 'relaxing' and 'funeral dirge' and, unfortunately, you just crossed the line." Seriously, I'm deeply grateful to Debbie for her music selections that are such an integral part of our healthy experience.

Experts from all walks of life—from Plato and Florence Nightingale to the drummer for the Grateful Dead—all agree on the healthy contribution that music makes.[16] We're even told that "pregnant women listening to music during labor are only half as likely to need anesthesia!"[17] Research results on listening to your iPod during a painful PowerPoint delivery are still pending.

We know from research and personal experience that music can heighten our emotions as it immerses us in multimedia experiences. It can instantly uplift our spirits and speed the healing of our bodies. But, bottom line, can music raise test scores?

One wonders if that isn't part of the motivation for one middle school in suburban Sacramento, California, that opened its 2010–2011 school year music program with students playing No. 2 pencils instead of musical instruments. School officials claim that budget cuts led to the decision,[18] but I'll be watching test scores to determine if spending six weeks playing a pencil like a flute or a clarinet doesn't give those student "musicians" an unfair advantage when it comes to wielding the No. 2 pencils on upcoming standardized tests.

I might be kidding about watching the Sacramento test scores but I'm definitely serious about anything that can help our students—and our workshop and conference session attendees—to remember what we are presenting not only for any looming tests but also for any beyond-the-test applications of the information and lessons. The good news is that music *can* help with memory *if*—the research tells us—we control certain factors.

First, the music that is played (encoded) during learning needs to be the *same* music that is played (decoded) during the recall test. Recall is worse if different music is played or if music is played during learning but not during testing.[19]

Note: Too bad for students studying with music if that same music won't be playing during the test. Although this certainly raises the question—with the ubiquitous presence of iPods—as to whether students could choose their own music to study with *and* listen to during the test. That would be a fun, albeit cacophonous, research project!

Second, the *tempo* of the music should be the same. If the same piece of music played for learning is played at a different speed during testing, that would result in worse, not better, recall.[20] Of course, using the same recording of the music both times would alleviate this potential problem.

Third, it helps if the *mood* of the topic matches the mood of the music. Positive words are better remembered if heard during happy music and recall is better for negative words heard during sad music.[21]

For example, think of the mournful piece "Ashokan Farewell," which Ken Burns uses as the title theme for his *Civil War* series. It is also played while reading the 1861 letter from Sullivan Ballou to his wife, Sarah. That exquisitely poignant letter is all the more unforgettable with the haunting music in the background.

On a more cheerful and whimsical note, think of the alphabet song. I had the privilege of volunteering with second-language learners at Scott Lane Elementary School in Santa Clara, California. Besides my small-group tutoring, the K–2 students also had the benefit of the *Waterford Early Reading Program*,[22] which included several catchy alphabet songs. I happened to be present in May when a shy little boy named Chris was being tested on his progress for the year. He was answering the questions but in a whisper and with downcast eyes. Then the teacher-tester asked him if he knew the alphabet. All of a sudden the head lifted up, the chest puffed out, and Chris sang from A to Z at the top of his lungs. Quite proud of himself, to say the least!

We also know from our own life experience that any time music is played during an *emotionally charged* event, we will remember both the event and the song more vividly. A humorous example I like to use during my presentations is from an episode of *The Cosby Show*. Claire (Phylicia Rashad) asks Cliff (Bill Cosby) what he said to her when he proposed. He's obviously struggling with his response. But when she follows up with: "What was playing on the car radio when you gave me the ring?" He replies, without missing a beat: "Ray Charles. 'I Can't Stop Loving You.' Sold fourteen million copies. Now deal with that!"

Activity 8.6

Think of an emotionally charged event in your life—good or bad. Can you remember the music that was playing? Think of a presentation you have coming up. What piece of music might be appropriate to play along with part of that presentation? Why?

In the classroom or a multisession training, remember that not all the music needs to come from the teacher or the presenter. Find ways for students and participants to demonstrate musically their understanding and mastery of the course and workshop content:

- Instead of reading a book report from the book jacket, why not perform a musical book share? In a video that Bruce Campbell put together some years back on *Multiple Intelligences in the Classroom*,[23] he included a wonderful clip of student Leah Orr, from Skyline Junior High School, based on two books (*The Upstairs Room* and *The Journey Back* by Johanna Reiss) about two Jewish girls who were hiding during World War II. Leah sings a cappella about "a scared little girl, hiding her identity, scared to be the enemy, fighting for her life. One little girl, hated by the outside world." When I play this in my presentations, a hush descends on the room. When I ask whether Leah "got" the books, every head in the audience nods. She didn't just parrot back a summary of the content. She took the essential threads and wove them into her own musical tapestry.

- A group project might use the Simple Truths *Great Quotes Movie*[24] as a model to demonstrate the essence of its learning of a particular topic or unit of study. (Experience the powerful movie yourself, either online or by purchasing the DVD from Simple Truths.) The idea would be to create a series of slides— each with a photographic image and a powerful quotation—and put the whole presentation to emotionally charged and appropriate instrumental music.

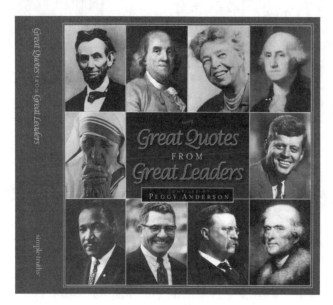

Musical experiences enrich learning for all the participants and they honor the gifts of musically inclined learners who contribute to those experiences. How many people show up to your classes or trainings with an iPod full of music? How many of them, if encouraged to do so, might share something with you during a break that could be perfect to introduce your next segment or review what you just presented? How many of your students might have undiscovered gifts? Like square pegs in the round holes of your educational system. Like Elvis Presley, who was not allowed to sing in the choir of his high school in Tupelo, Mississippi. Or two of the future Beatles who lay fallow in a classroom in Liverpool, England, their talent totally unrecognized. Who knew? Who asked?

Fortunately, today there are school districts that create magnet schools where students gifted in music (and other fine and performing arts) can flourish. My nephew (brother Wes's son Tor) was homeschooled in middle school because the public school system was just not working for him. All of that changed when he enrolled in TSOTA, Tacoma Public Schools' high school Tacoma School of the Arts. All of a sudden, everything made sense.

With access to state-of-the-art equipment for sound engineering, for the first time, school was where Tor wanted to be. And the enthusiasm spilled over to subjects other than music. The first week of school Tor called me long distance, all excited: "Did you know, Aunt Lynell, that physics is all about music?" (Pythagoras had figured that out before Tor but in the centuries that intervened, schools had somehow lost sight of that wisdom.)

After three years at TSOTA, Tor went on to major in sound engineering at a specialty school in Norway. From there he was recruited to attend the prestigious Liverpool Institute for Performing Arts (LIPA)— founded by Sir Paul McCartney, who wanted future students to have better educational opportunities in that old school building than he had received.

Whether you are blessed to work in a TSOTA or a LIPA, or whether your calling is to travel from school to school or conference to conference, the mission and the intention are the same. We want to make the time spent with us a gift to remember. What better way to do that than to encourage our students and audience members to hone *their* special gifts. Some may need our help to identify their gifts. Others, such as Tor, have already figured out that "it's *all* about music" and just need us to give them access to the best instruments and the opportunities for guided practice and performance.

Now some of you may be operating under more challenging conditions. Maybe as a classroom teacher, the music department at your school—if it hasn't been disbanded altogether—has pencils for drumsticks and you personally can't carry a tune in a bucket. Maybe as a presenter, you're still trying to figure out how to download music from YouTube and get it to play in your PowerPoint, and, honestly, before reading this chapter you thought that music was just something used to annoy people in elevators. But now, as a dedicated professional, you are determined to be as masterful with music as you are with images.

- You want a music track to accompany your lessons and presentations so you can open the free-flowing channel for learning and have people humming and singing both during and after your class or session. (Remember to encourage clapping, too. Presenters, like musicians, thrive on applause.)

- You understand that whatever music you choose will affect your listeners' health along with their emotions so you will make your selections thoughtfully, responsibly, and intentionally. (If necessary, don a stethoscope or scrubs to get in the right mood.)

- You've reviewed the research findings and know that to get the maximum educational benefits from using music, you need to use the *same* music (and at the *same* tempo) when you try to *recall* material as when you work to *learn* it. ("You put your right foot *in*—you put your right foot *out*." Same foot. Sure. Go ahead and "Shake it." "That's what it's all about.")

- You recognize that even if you are a consummate musician (who knew?) you are not the only source of music in the room. Share the microphone. Know that today all teenagers (and increasing numbers of educators) come equipped with mobile music devices (this month it's iPods) loaded with more songs than you can shake a No. 2 pencil at. And they love to share their music. Find a way to make that facility with music a plus in assignments that you give them. (Even during a short presentation, in small groups, one person can "rap to review" for the others something he or she has learned in the last ten minutes.)

- You look and listen for the Elvises, the Beatles, and the Tors in your classroom or audience. You improvise or "jam" with them to orchestrate emotional connections, to weave music through your content in memorable ways, to shift and lift your students' and audiences' moods, and to do it all quickly.

Sometimes we only have an hour. No time to waste.

9

Tapping emotion

Have you ever tried to save money by buying a generic brand of sticky notes? Did you end up (as I did) throwing them in the garbage because they just didn't stick? For the sticky notes that work, Post-it notes, 3M holds the patent (and the secret) for the stickiness. For presentations that work, come closer so I can whisper the secret in your ear: *Emotions stick!* Like mental Post-it notes, they tell your brain to "pay attention! You're going to want to remember this!"[1]

It doesn't matter which emotion—any positive or negative emotion has sticking potential. For a rich source of commonly used emotional words, consult Karol K. Truman's *Feelings Buried Alive Never Die,* which lists 759 negative words alongside their positive antidotes.[2]

Activity 9.1

Contemplate this short selection from Truman's list. First, look at a negative feeling, then the positive feelings that could replace it. Imagine how the different attitudes would play out between you and your audience during a presentation, between you and your students on a typical school day.

If you are in a class, get into groups of three and pick one feeling—positive or negative—to dramatize in a one-minute skit. Have four or five groups volunteer to perform. See if the rest of the class or audience can guess which feeling or emotion is being portrayed. Rely as much on body gestures and facial expressions as on the words you express. (Remember that humor is always appreciated.)

Feeling words

Negative	Positive
Apathetic	Concerned, caring
Bored	Excited, interested, involved
Complaining	Approving, appreciative, grateful, enjoying
Deceitful	Honest, honorable, true
Fearful	Confident, assured, resolute, brave
Grouchy	Contented, good-natured, cheerful, happy
Hurtful	Sensitive to others, caring, kind, loving
Rude	Gracious, kind, considerate, courteous
Sloppy	Neat, tidy, organized, particular
Tired	Energetic, vigorous, vital, alert, peppy

What feelings are emanating from you when you teach or present? If, as speaker-blogger Seth Godin alleges, presentations are about "the transfer of emotion,"[3] what emotions are you emoting to persuade your audience to adopt your point of view? Godin continues: "Our brains have two sides. The right side is emotional, musical, and moody. The left side is focused on dexterity, facts, and hard data."[4] Which side should you appeal to if you want to make what Godin calls an "emotional sale"?[5]

A colleague explained his approach as follows:

> Instead of starting with the statistics on growing use of cell phones, I start with a picture of my granddaughter at eighteen months old—yes, I know she's adorable—already glued to a cell phone.

> The image conjures up feelings that set the stage for the numbers I will drop on the audience next. (There are already 4.1 billion cell phone users in the world, and, in two years. . . .)

What do you think of that approach? Can we all agree that if we *started* with the "numbers" 99 percent of the audience would either tune out or walk out? (In classrooms, when walking out is not an option, all 99 percent would just tune out.) But does prefacing the numbers with an image—even a really good image—suffice to keep the audience's attention once we leave the image for the data?

Before you answer that last question, consider a research project involving the Save the Children foundation.[6] The researchers wanted to see how people responded to an appeal to make a charitable contribution to an abstract cause versus a single person. They offered each participant five one-dollar bills. The researchers then tested two request letters. The first featured all the *statistics* about the enormity of the problems facing starving children in Africa. The second offered information about a seven-year-old girl named Rokia, from Mali, Africa.

Food, hygiene, medical care, and education—"*Her* life will be changed for forever as a result of *your* gift."

Participants who read the statistics letter gave an average of $1.14 (from the five dollars they had available). Those who read about Rokia contributed $2.38—more than twice as much.

Now here's where the research gets really interesting. A third group was given *both* letters. They could read the statistics to see the enormity of the problem *and* they could read about Rokia's individual needs. They gave an average of $1.43—almost a dollar less than those who got the Rokia story alone.

The researchers' conclusion? Reading the statistics shifted the participants into an analytical frame of mind—away from the emotional response to Rokia that inspired them to donate in the first place.[7]

Activity 9.2

Think of data, numbers, or statistics that you would like to communicate in a memorable, right-brained way to an audience or a classroom full of students. Find a way to use emotions to communicate your point in addition to the actual data. If you are in a class, get into groups of three to discuss and then and share your group's best strategies with the rest of the class.

Not all solutions involve PowerPoint or other technology-assisted approaches. On their neurolearning blog, Fernette and Brock Eide recently shared that "tweaking subjects with humor or emotional content may suddenly turn an impossible-to-learn subject doable." Working with the learning disabled, they have observed many low-tech ideas that work: making up funny associations or wordplays, talking aloud with funny cartoon voices, singing material to the tune of a popular song, or even just standing on a chair. (A change of perspective never hurts.) One time in their clinic, the Eides recount, they saw an older dyslexic child who for years had reversed his letters and numbers. When they asked him how he finally got things straight, he grinned and replied: "I just found out that I had to give the letters and numbers different personalities like 'nasty number nine.' If the information somehow touches you personally, you'll remember it."[8] And, as history has shown, act on it.

One of the most powerful examples of that—and one that I would strongly encourage administrators to share with their teachers and teachers to share with their students—is the collection of child labor photographs taken by Lewis W. Hine.[9] Sixty-nine captioned photos are available to download for educational use.

Hine did not editorialize. He simply took the photographs and stated the facts in his captions.

Newsboy: Michael McNeils, age 8 [seen with photographer Hine]. The boy has just recovered from his second attack of pneumonia. Was found selling papers in a big rainstorm. Philadelphia, Pennsylvania.

As a teacher at the Ethical Culture School in New York City, Hine encouraged his students to use photography as an educational medium. In 1908, he left his teaching position to work full time as the

photographer for the National Child Labor Committee (NCLC). Over
the next decade Hine documented child labor in America to aid the
NCLC's lobbying efforts to end the practice. His photos revealed the
heart-wrenching stories: a little boy working in a textile mill on the
same machine his brother had been killed falling into the day before.
(He was given the morning off to attend the funeral.) A girl whose
mother had braided her hair. (The child's friend had caught her long,
loosely flowing hair in the machinery the day before and had almost
been killed.) A boy, fortunate enough to have boots, working in the glass
factory. (Most children worked barefoot.)

With his camera as the tool, Hine was instrumental in changing the
child labor laws in the United States.

A word of warning to K–12 classroom teachers: Hine had to stop
taking the pictures because the children's stories were breaking his
heart. You and your more tenderhearted students may have a similar
reaction. Also, there is one section of the collection that covers the
illegal activities that cost the teenage boys whatever little money they
had earned. That might be inappropriate content for K–12 classrooms.
So, although I usually encourage students to access primary sources,
in this case my recommendation would be for the teacher to download
select images (and captions) rather than sending the students to the site
themselves.

Activity 9.3

Identify something in your community that could be changed for the better. Use a camera to take a compelling image (or series of images) of the egregious situation. Write a caption that doesn't judge, just states the facts.

Alternatively, find a photograph in a newspaper, journal, or online news-reporting site that takes this approach.

Note: This can be a life-changing experience for students and for those around them who are compelled to act when they see the images.

Besides the traditional media outlets, of course, today great emotionally charged stories are also popping up on YouTube. A case in point is Dave Carroll's "United Breaks Guitars." After a yearlong saga of writing letters seeking restitution for his irreparably damaged Taylor (expensive) guitar, Dave decided to take his case to a more public forum. Along with almost nine million other people, you have probably seen the music video of his tale of woe and sung along with its euphonious refrain: "United, you broke my Taylor guitar. United, some big help you are. You broke it, you should fix it. You're liable, just admit it. I should have flown with someone else or gone by car. 'Cause United breaks guitars."

Dave is a talented—and delightfully funny—musician. The original tune is catchy; the words clearly paint the story and are artfully complemented by the hysterical video that Dave's friends helped him put together. You feel for him—especially when you see the alleged indifference of the United employees and the chalk outline of what *was* his precious guitar.

The whole video is a masterpiece. Of course, United Airlines had a change of heart and at Carroll's request, made a donation to a charity that provides music education to underprivileged children. I heard they have also adopted his video for training in their customer service department.[10]

My point in sharing Dave's story is that it exemplifies what we need to do as educators and presenters. We've tried the traditional left-brained approaches. Wrote the letters. Cited the statistics. But, guess what? It didn't work for Dave. It doesn't work for us. Or our students.

Students' most powerful work also comes from the heart. In Los Angeles, California, when a middle-school teacher asked her students to write short poems as iMovies, a girl named Jasmin put her words to the background music of Selena's *No Me Queda Mas* (There's nothing left for me). She told of a bad situation at home and tearfully confessed that she felt like screaming when she saw her parents fighting.

It should not be surprising that children who are "emotionally distracted, upset and preoccupied by the explosive drama of their own family lives, are unable to concentrate on such mundane matters as multiplication tables."[11] As John Medina reports, "Kids whose parents fight get lower grades. They also do worse on standardized math and reading tests."[12]

Might there be people in your classroom—or in your presentation audience—like Jasmin? Going through any kind of pain in their lives? Are your words encouraging and uplifting? Positive and healing?

What if someone were to tally the words in your presentation into two columns—positive and negative—which column would receive more tally marks? (Once you get ten tally marks, drop down to the next cell.)

Negative	Positive

Time for a little fantasy. Imagine that your ATM fairy just gave you a huge stack of money. (You had attempted to withdraw twenty dollars. She gave you twenty thousand.) Over your squeals of delight, you hear her Godlike voice saying, "This is your money, my dear. Now take it into the bank and—your choice—ask them to *deposit* or *withdraw* it from your account."

"Excuse me, ATM fairy," you say, "but do you think I'm crazy? Of course, I want to *deposit!*"

"You are no more crazy, my dear, than the millions of other people who take the thousands of *words* I give them every day and bank them as debits rather than credits. You see, comments with a positive emotional charge energize and enrich our lives and put resources into our reserve account; comments with a negative emotional charge drain us and leave us vulnerable to every 'virus' that comes along. There is no neutral column. You have to decide where to make the entries. By the way, it isn't just your *words.* I've noticed you are embedding video clips in your PowerPoints. Some of the humor leans toward the negative and the sarcastic. A real drain on your account. Try finding some vintage Red Skelton or Danny Kaye videos instead. Better to laugh yourself silly than laugh yourself sick."

Sometimes those ATM fairies get a bit opinionated and more than a little preachy but maybe she did have a point. Actually, she reminded me of story I heard in a wonderful workshop that I took with Dick Bolles (author of *What Color Is Your Parachute?*). Dick shared with us that our hearts know the words we want to hear. He explained that even though he is a writer, he could never write about nuclear bomb parts, say, or medieval instruments of torture. It's his passion for a specific content area—career and mission planning—that inspires his gift for written expression.

To bring this point home, Dick gave each of us a wonderful resource: *The Random House Webster's Word Menu.*[13] This book—a combination dictionary, thesaurus, and almanac—organizes language by subject matter rather than by the traditional decontextualized alphabetical listing. Dick invited us to leaf through the book and find pages that contained words we would want to hear at work on a daily basis.

Fancying myself something of a computer geek, I went straight for the "Science and Technology" section. Although words such as *CPU,* *computer,* and *RAM* were familiar, they weren't particularly inspiring. Moving on to "Institutions: Social Sciences: Education," again the terms were familiar and some even tugged at the heartstrings. But it was on reading the words listed under "The Human Condition: Faith: Truth, Wisdom, and Spiritual Attainment" that involuntary tears started pouring down my cheeks. Words like *awe, forgiveness, grace, harmony, numinous, peace, radiance, splendor,* and *vision* felt like a calling.[14]

I came out of that exercise knowing that the content of my future writing and presentations, although ostensibly about technology and education, would at their core be about ways to improve the human condition.

There is no right or wrong answer in the *Word Menu* book; it is simply a tool that we can use to identify our highest calling. I have often recommended it to high school and college teachers to share with those students who seem to be wandering in the dark. It just might shine the light on a life's path for them and give them the vision they need to pursue studies related to advancing on that path.

Activity 9.4

Make a list of ten positive words that are abstract concepts you would like students to understand before they leave school. Arrange them in priority order and make them into a Wordle (or some other word cloud or visual representation of word frequency).[15]

This Wordle was constructed from the words supplied by good friends of mine—clearly folks with good hearts!

Another, more readily available source for these powerful words is the list compiled by Gerald Grow in his *Words worth 1000 pictures*.[16]

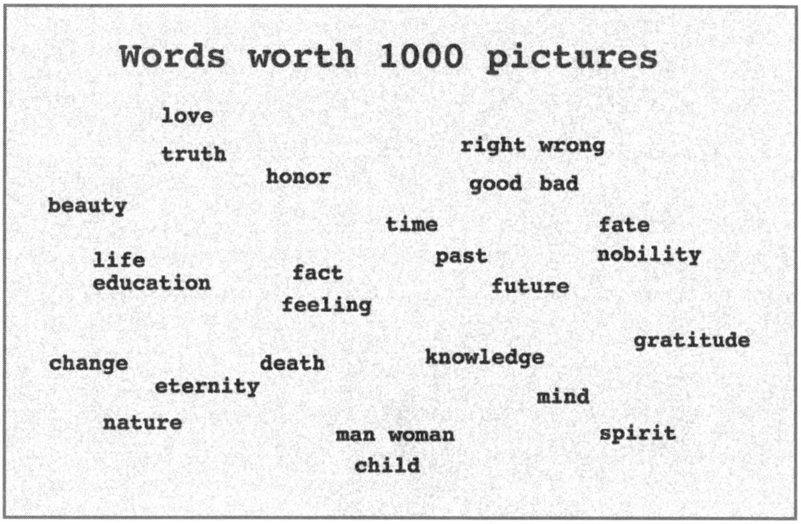

Words worth 1000 pictures

love

truth

right wrong

honor

good bad

beauty

time

fate

life

past

nobility

education

fact

future

feeling

gratitude

change

death

knowledge

eternity

mind

nature

man woman

spirit

child

Activity 9.5

Choose one positive emotion word. Discuss your own mental images for that word.

Create a ten- to twelve-slide PowerPoint of full-screen images illustrating that word. (Adding music would be a nice touch.) Post your slideshow to www.slideshare.com or just share it with your class.

Note: Make sure all your images are photographs you have taken (and made copyright free) or are listed under a Creative Commons license.

If you are working in a classroom, by all means assign Activity 9.5 to your students. (They would not have to post their slideshows to Slideshare, although that is a nice habit to teach them.) When you have to find the pictures (rather than looking at someone else's), it creates a deeper emotional impact.

I learned this firsthand recently during one of those "What do you do for a living?" chitchats with a new acquaintance. I tried to explain how I help people—mainly educators—create more powerful presentations by replacing the usual screens of bulleted text with compelling, full-screen photographic images. He nodded and inquired

"So, do you have an image for love?"

Caught a bit off-guard, I answered with the question: "Do you?"

Without missing a beat, he replied: "A castle keep."

I smiled knowingly and when I got home the first thing I did was Google *castle keep*. Turns out it's the innermost sanctuary of the castle, the place where valuables are guarded and that is defended to the death.

Besides this wonderful image—which definitely enriched my understanding of the potential depths of *love*—he gave me the incentive to plumb my heart for my own, intensely personal image. A few days and several tears later, I realized that my image for *love* was a rose with early morning dewdrops.

Why? Because the people who have loved me unconditionally have all shown their love by acts of service. Like the rose, which doesn't even have to ask for the dew, I was blessed with their tender care.

Now imagine a long hallway at your school or workplace with dozens, maybe hundreds of images of *love*—each with a caption explaining why the person posted that image. Could those images give students a richer, deeper understanding of the potential of *love,* a concept that would go behind the shallow flirtations and sexual denouements that pass for love in music videos, television, and the silver screen?

And what about *kindness*? Could some visual reminders of *kindness* change the ambiance in a school? Reverse the bullying trend? Forge bonds between students? Even create a generation that could imagine problem-solving strategies other than violence or war?

Besides *love* and *kindness,* what other words would you choose to illustrate? My good friend and treasured colleague Jerome Burg just sent me a movie of his grandson laughing. It rippled through me like a health tonic—without the bad taste. Thanks, Jerome, for reminding us to put *laughter* on our list and keep it gurgling in our hearts.

Activity 9.6

Find a partner (your mirror if you are reading this alone or a small child if you have access to one) and say to that beautiful person in front of you:

"You make me laugh. Thanks."

A little chuckle would provide a nice touch, punctuation, if you will, after the word *thanks.*

Regarding all these positive words—I hope you are still chuckling because it's good for your health—there is some really good news.

Science has finally proved what we educators have always known in our hearts: whatever emotion we are feeling will reverberate throughout our classroom or presentation venue. I don't want to spoil our mood—chuckle, chuckle—so I'll send you to the HeartMath website[17] for the hard data. Let me just share an image from *The HeartMath Solution*[18] (book) that I have found to be particularly inspirational and a great way to illustrate the HeartMath research in my presentations.

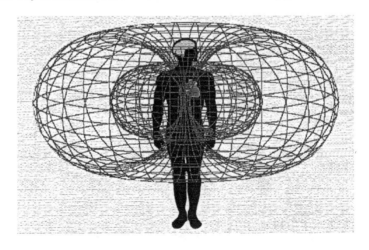

Whatever you are "thinking" in your heart radiates at least fifteen feet in every direction. A teacher standing in the middle of a thirty-by-thirty-foot classroom thinking, "I really love these kids," becomes a classroom-sized "love doughnut." A presenter, appreciating the participants who have shown up that day, can use the ten or fifteen minutes before the presentation begins to walk purposefully throughout the audience, easily changing the mood of the group and setting the tone for the session. You do not need to announce this (or put "Love Doughnut" on your business cards) because it works on a subconscious level. Your class, your audiences? They won't know how you did it; they'll just know that they feel better when they leave your class or presentation than when they came in.

Remember our little secret: *emotions stick!* The words we choose tally up and contribute to the impact we make. The heart behind those words even more so. As they say with a Scottish brogue, 'tis more felt than telt.

Keep this in mind not only as you choose the *words* for your lessons and presentations, but also as you search for *images* and *music* and all the other elements that carry the content from your heart to theirs.

It's easy to get caught up in the negative images that bombard us—the sensational local, national, and world news that screams at us about natural disasters, murders, politicians (and other public figures) behaving badly, wars, and other gory acts of inhumanity.[19]

In the relatively short time that we have students in our care (and the even shorter time that we have audiences in our presentations), we need to counteract with *positive* images, images to uplift the weary and heal the walking wounded. We need to find jewels such as Van Gogh's *Sunflowers.*

Just looking at this painting can boost your immune system for six hours![20] (You definitely want the color version on your desktop!) History records that Van Gogh painted four sunflowers canvases with a heart full of gratitude for the friendship of Paul Gauguin, who was coming to visit him in the south of France. Van Gogh himself referred to them as his "gratitude paintings." In ways I do not pretend to understand, the loving gratitude in the painter's heart has become part of the paintings. When we look at them we feel the gratitude and we are healed by the presence of that emotion in our own hearts.

This might explain the delight we experience—how absolutely great we feel—when we go out into nature. As people of faith might wonder, are we in some mysterious way feeling the love of the Creator when we enjoy the tapestry of the creation?

Most certainly as teachers and presenters we know we can and we must take the opportunity to create a databank of positive, healing images that our students and our audiences can take with them for life. Images of loyalty, kindness, truth, beauty, love, and—most of all—hope, hope for their future.

Telling stories

My cousin Sandy, my brother Wes, and I spent every weekend together the whole time we were growing up. Our mothers (sisters by birth) devised the clever scheme to save Sandy from growing up as an only child (and to have some alone time with their respective husbands) by shipping off the kid(s) every other weekend. Auntie Vera was a fabulous cook, Uncle Berger was a teddy bear, and their house had a basement full of fun nooks and crannies, so Wes and I always enjoyed our stay. What I remember most vividly from those weekends was Wes always bugging Sandy and me to tell him stories—as if two girls with dolls and coloring books had nothing better to do. His demand still rings in our ears: "You hasta tell me a story!"

Actually, Wes and I were both sponges for stories. Whenever we were at our house, Dad read us a story every night. (He also sang to us but I'll spare you the details on that inadvertently humorous effort.) And then there was our other part-time caregiver, Grandma Burmark. She was a large Norwegian woman with a wonderful assemblage of built-in pillows that enveloped Wes and me as we settled into her lap to hear her stories. We could never get enough. Mom and Dad would always come home to find the three of us asleep in the rocking chair. Most of the time, I think Grandma fell asleep first but Wes and I were so comfortable that we soon followed.

Last month, I was at cousin Sandy's house and no sooner did I sit down than her granddaughter was in my lap demanding: "Tell me a story!" Sandy and I had a good laugh when I replied, "You mean, 'You hasta tell me a story!'?"

Children aren't shy about asking for stories. When a hot-line service gave local elementary school kids a toll-free phone number to call in case they got scared being home alone after school, I heard one little girl inquire: "If I call that number, will somebody read me a story?"

As adults, we aren't as vocal (or maybe even conscious) about it but we still prefer to get new information in the form of stories. At our conferences, the keynote speakers we enjoy the most are the best storytellers. I'm not sure the conference organizers understand this. They look for people who are famous, whose names or positions will be a "draw" to the conference. What they too often neglect to verify is whether those speakers—away from their home turf and without a script—can tell a compelling story that will resonate with educators.

Conference programs continue to advertise "engaging" presenters offering "interactive" presentations. My colleague Gary Stager quips that "interactive" has come to mean that the audience is still breathing. Maybe, Gary might suggest, instead of breathalyzers, we need to measure audience engagement with a more finely tuned instrument, say an fMRI (functional magnetic resonance imaging) machine?

Funny thing, a new study from Princeton University has done just that! Researchers took fMRI scans of people's brains as they listened to a woman recounting a story and the scans showed that *the listeners' brain patterns tracked those of the storyteller almost exactly.* In most cases they lagged one to three seconds behind; but in some cases the brain patterns even preceded those of the storyteller![1] "Participants' brains became intimately coupled, mirroring that of the speaker," says Uri Hasson, lead researcher on the project.[2]

We've all experienced this kind of synchronization. Think of songs or rhymes where we anticipate the word at the end of the line:

> Twinkle, twinkle, little star.
> How I wonder where you _____.
> Up above the world so high,
> Like a diamond in the _____.

And we've all had those moments during conversations with family members, colleagues, or close friends when we can finish one another's sentences. We've attended presentations where we were drifting, drifting, praying to stay awake . . . and then the presenter shifted into story mode and we were mercifully back up, erect and alert in our seats.

Hasson continues, "Listeners who were paying attention and who understood the story . . . were also judged to be the best at retelling the tale."[3]

As teachers and presenters, if we want our students and audiences to stay awake during our presentation and to be able to recall and apply the information in it, we need to do two things:

1. Get their attention

2. Present our information in the form of *stories* they can understand

Getting their attention, as discussed in previous chapters, can be as easy as playing music or displaying a compelling image (or series of images) on the screen as they enter the room. Or it can be starting right out with a story, as my colleague and longtime friend Sara Armstrong[4] frequently does. No time wasted. She has attendees hanging on her every word from the very beginning of the presentation. And that opening story serves as the anchor for the rest of the session. One story has coalesced what could have been an incohesive group and has given it a shared vision as the basis of the work it is going to do together. The stories are simple, yet profound; timely, yet timeless.

Can you relate to the following high-school-reunion conversation?

Classmate: So, Lynell, who was your favorite teacher?

Lynell: Miss Schmidt. Fourth grade. Every day, after lunch, she read us stories. What about you? Who was your favorite teacher?

Classmate: Mr. Rich. Eighth-grade history. Remember? He read us stories.

Lynell: Yeah, he was great! What about high school?

Classmate: Didn't really like high school.

But, come on. Aren't the teachers who tell stories somehow less serious about their content? Trying to win some kind of popularity contest? Not prepared and just using the stories to fill up class time that could be used to really buckle down and learn the material in time for the standardized test?

Before you answer that, let me ask you to check whether the stories involve a big gray dog or rented white frosting.

Big gray dog? What's obvious when we talk about illustrating with pictures is also true when we illustrate with stories. Consider a student who is creating a digital story about a *sad little white dog*. On his opening slide he displays a picture of a *happy big gray dog*. Got lazy? Needs better search skills? Gave up? In the same way that we need to spend time reflecting on which picture we choose to display, we need to wrestle with which story we select to tell.[5]

Rented white frosting? When I was sixteen, Mom, Dad, and I went to a wedding. (Somehow, Wes escaped the event.) I don't remember the ceremony, but I'll never forget the reception. Dad and I immediately spotted the magnificent cake and were salivating at the thought of each getting a piece with the frosting roses on it. 9:30. 10:30. They still hadn't cut the cake. Mom wanted to leave but Dad and I both said that we were not about to go home without our piece of cake! A guest sitting at the same table overheard us and said, "You didn't know? They just rented the frosting. There's only cardboard inside. No cake."

The stories your teachers told you when you were in school, the stories you tell today to your students and the teachers and other educators who come to your presentations—are they gray dogs (off topic) or white dogs (to the point)? Do they offer rented frosting (fluffy teasers) or actual cake (real substance)? Either way, good stories—by their very nature— are going to grip our listeners. *Why* do we remember stories? Because stories are *how* we remember. As Jason Ohler explains:

> I have come to believe, on a very basic level that feels bio-logical to me, that we need stories. Without them, life is just too overwhelming to piece together from scratch each day. Stories allow us to take snippets of life and put them together in ways that make it possible for us to learn and remember new things.
>
> While this quality (this utility as an information organizer) has always been a hallmark of stories, it's particularly poi-gnant now because we desperately need tools to navigate and coordinate the immense amount of information available to us.[6]

At the most basic level, the listeners, our audiences, our students are urging, "Tell us stories about your world to help us make sense of our own."

They aren't coming to us for slide after slide of statistical data or to be impressed by the depth and breadth of our knowledge. They have Google for that, if they are really interested. What they need from us is the conversion of facts (information) into wisdom (story), placing what we have to share in a context that is meaningful, instructional, and even inspirational.

The material we select (which ten sites we cherry-pick from the eight million that Google offers us) and the context we create are going to be determined not only by our desire to keep the information suc-cinct and relevant, but also by our propensity to share what we sub-consciously judge to be the most in line with our own personal belief system, the soil in which our own flowers are planted. Think of the hydrangea:

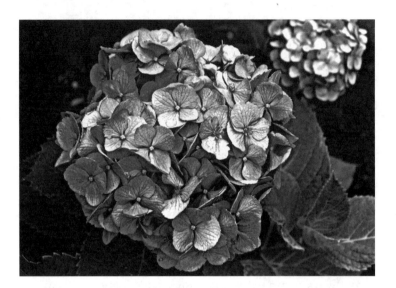

The same beautiful flowers will turn blue or pink according to the soil in which the bush is planted.

Activity 10.1

Pretend you are reporting on the 2010 oil spill in the Gulf of Mexico. Whom would you interview to find out what happened? How would the story be different if coming from a spokesperson for British Petroleum versus an independent businessperson shrimp fishing off the coast of Louisiana?

If you are a classroom teacher, you might try this activity with students. In groups of three, have one person be the newscaster and the other two be representatives of opposing sides of the story. The topic could be something timely in the local, national, or international news; a controversy at school (for example, starting times, school uniforms or dress code, pizza on the breakfast menu, and so on); or historical battles (for example, North versus South in the Civil War).

Granted, different people will have different perspectives on a policy or an event. But what if you took a photograph? Photographers might shoot from different angles (literally and figuratively) but surely those *viewing* the picture would all *see* the same, intended message, don't you think? Let's test this theory with an activity I call the *Progressive Story*.

Depending on the age of the students, the complexity of the topic, and the time allocated in your presentations and workshops for the activity, you might decide to use anywhere from four to sixteen images. (The nine slides shown here worked perfectly with a classroom of fourth-graders.)

If you'd like to use the slideshow whose black-and-white thumbnails are shown here, feel free to use the PowerPoint titled "Streets of Sunnyvale" provided on the DVD that accompanies this book.

Activity 10.2

For your class or presentation, project a slideshow of four to sixteen full-screen, full-color photographic images for the entire group to see.

Divide the class or audience into groups of three and give a small, soft ball (commonly referred to as a Koosh ball) to the person in each group with the shortest hair. That person starts the story by telling something about the first image on the screen and then tosses the Koosh ball to another person in the group, who continues the story by narrating the second slide. And so on.

Make sure everyone in the group participates. Remember that great humor makes a great story and that heartfelt emotions make it memorable.

Take time for all the participants to give themselves a round of applause.

Note (to teachers and trainers): The first time I did this activity was in a conference ballroom with 450 people. Twelve images and one Koosh ball. How many people actively participated? Thirteen. (The twelve who contributed to the story and the one person who was accidentally hit on the head with the Koosh ball.) When it dawned on me to hand over the Koosh balls (and the control) to groups of three, I transformed this activity into one in which *everyone* participated!

Each group gets the same pictures. Do you think every group comes up with the same story? Anywhere *near* the same story? If the random pattern of laughter, applause, and high-fives erupting throughout the audience is any indication, I would judge that the different groups are creating very different stories!

And all the while, their brains are frolicking in Velcroland—making connections, hooking new images onto the loops of previous story lines. Or, as a cognitive scientist would phrase it: "Most of our experience, our knowledge, and our thinking is organized as stories."[7] The power of the progressive story is that participants process this notion as a concrete experience rather than hearing about it as an abstract concept.

As Chip and Dan Heath argue so persuasively in their *New York Times* best seller *Made to Stick,* "concreteness sticks."[8] The classic example is the Nordstrom clothing and shoe store. Management could simply have told its employees that their mission was to provide "the best customer service in the industry." But, as the Heaths point out, this just "sounds like something that JCPenney or Sears might tell *its* employees." To make the message stick—to turn Nordstrom employees into "Nordies," into customer-service zealots—required spreading stories, concrete examples such as the following:

- The Nordie who ironed a shirt for a customer who needed it for a meeting that afternoon

- The Nordie who cheerfully gift-wrapped products a customer bought at a rival Macy's store

- The Nordie who refunded money for a set of tires—even though Nordstrom doesn't sell tires[9]

As teachers and presenters, how easy is it for us to slip into abstract speak, to chant those strings of words we have paid consultants so much money to alliterate for us? Actually, those of us who've been around education long enough don't even need the consultants. We are more than capable of spinning the jargon ourselves. To prove the point, take a moment to whip out the following assignment. (If you're new to education, find an administrator to help you.)

Activity 10.3

Write a fifty-word policy for the personnel manual on providing academic support to homebound or hospitalized students in your school district. Be sure to use words like *rigor*, *standards*, and *implementation*.

Imagine the impact of reading that new policy at the next staff meeting versus the impact of telling the following story:

> A retired schoolteacher had volunteered to visit and teach young children at a large hospital. One day, the phone rang and she received her first assignment. On the other end of the line was the classroom teacher of a young boy who had been studying nouns and adverbs before he had been hospitalized.
>
> It was not until the visiting teacher arrived outside the boy's room that she realized he was a patient in the hospital's burn unit. She was prepared to teach English grammar; she was not prepared to witness the horrible look and smell of badly burned human flesh.
>
> But something inside kept her from walking away, so she stumbled over to the bedside and stammered: "I'm the hospital teacher. Your teacher asked me to help you with your nouns and adverbs."
>
> The next morning when she came back to work with the boy, a nurse from the burn unit rushed up to her and asked: "What did you do to that boy?"

The teacher began to apologize profusely, but before she could finish, the nurse interrupted her: "You don't understand. His condition had been deteriorating over the past few days because he had given up hope. But ever since you were here with him yesterday, his whole attitude has changed. He's fighting back and responding to treatment. What did you do?"

When the nurse later questioned the little boy, he explained, "I figured I was gonna die until I saw that teacher." And, as a tear began to run down his little face, he concluded: "But when I saw her, I realized that they wouldn't bother sending a teacher to work on nouns and adverbs with a dying boy would they?"[10]

As presenters and as teachers, as experts in our field, we need to remember that to our audiences, our content—particularly the abstract verbal expression of it—is just a trunk of limp and lifeless puppets until we unfold the stage (context) and tug at the strings (emotion).

Speaking of puppets, have you seen The Great Philosophers[11] finger puppets? They are a great way to inspire storytelling from an anachronistic viewpoint. Get Galileo's take on global warming or have Thomas

Jefferson moderate a debate on farm subsidies. Use Leif Eriksson as a tour guide for a voyage on Google Earth or William Shakespeare to comment on love and marriage in twenty-first-century novels.

Activity 10.4

Try time-traveling in the other direction. Brainstorm historical scenarios—relevant to the content you present or teach—in which you could use one-way cell-phone conversations.

Columbus calling Queen Isabella to tell her he'd arrived in a rather strange looking India. Michelangelo calling his paint suppliers.

Note: For additional inspiration, consult *The Button-Down Mind of Bob Newhart*,[12] in which the actor conducts several one-sided phone conversations including "Abe Lincoln Versus Madison Avenue," when a slick promoter has to deal with the reluctance of the eccentric president to agree to the proposed efforts to boost his image.

One of the reasons these skits or stories work so well is that the brain is not fettered by verb tense. It is only too happy to watch Noah get his arc-building instructions on YouTube or Moses download the Ten Commandments from www.mountsinai.kjv. It is also why we can learn from the past and use those stories to inform our present and our future.

A big role of storytelling in education is learning lessons from the past. Whatever our content area, the topic of our presentation, we can save time and be more effective by citing a relevant story. Teaching about Lewis and Clark? Start with the wonderful video that includes an animated map of their journey and tells critical parts of the story in the voice of Sacagawea.[13]

How much more meaningful does the expedition become when students realize that its success was determined by a young girl—someone *their* age—who spoke the language of a potential enemy? I have watched Sacagawea's emotional reunion with her brother a hundred times. (I share it in many live presentations.) I still cry every time. So many lessons—not just United States history—could be spun off from that scene! We all need to be reminded that we have the power to change the course of history. We can be like Sacagawea and use our *connections* for good. We can be like Martin Luther King Jr. and use our *beliefs* for good.

Activity 10.5

Go *inside*. Think of an opportunity that you have to use one of your gifts for good. If you are a teacher, tell your students the story of Sacagawea and invite them to think about their own gifts and opportunities.

Presenters, trainers: find a way to incorporate this in your workshops. Your content will fall on deaf ears unless the listeners can use their own gifts to understand and incorporate your message with what they have to pass on.

The person who has given this idea of using your gifts the most thought is my friend and mentor Dick Bolles. He talks a lot about it in his book (and complementary workbook) *What Color Is Your Parachute?*[14] In his two-week workshop, he has participants complete a life-changing, life-orienting activity—"Skill Identification Through Stories"[15]—by writing seven stories as follows.

Part 1: Writing the story

Describe an episode in your life when you enjoyed yourself using skills that you may not have even realized you had to successfully overcome a problem. The more you go step by step and use the pronoun *I* (not *we*), the better. When you finish, underline or highlight the *verbs* and note them in the margin or in a parallel column right alongside where you demonstrated that skill in the story.

To give you an example, as a participant in Dick's seminar, here's the first story I wrote:

Skills	Story Title: CUE HVPA
was hired	In 1990, I was hired as the executive director of California's Computer Using Educators.
analyzed budget **calculated**	I analyzed the budget, noting there was only $25,000 in the bank. At $25 per member, the dues only produced $75,000 per year, and I calculated the expenses were at least three times that amount.
gathered info **estimated**	I gathered information on computer-using educators in the state and estimated there were at least 25,000 potential members for our association.
consulted friends **negotiated** **made money**	After I consulted friends in the computer business, I negotiated a high-volume purchase agreement (HVPA) between Apple Computer and CUE that made money for CUE when I
motivated	(1) motivated thousands of educators to pay $25 to join the organization to get the computer discount
negotiated **earned**	(2) negotiated rates with the bank and let it hold members' checks for forty-five days before turning the money over to Apple. (3) earned 2 percent interest on the "float."
designed, **produced**	I designed and produced an appealing brochure and order form.
persuaded to print, **distribute**	I persuaded Apple to print the brochures and the county offices of education to distribute 25,000 copies—all at no cost to CUE.
set up accounting procedures	I set up accounting procedures for logging in the money and passing on the orders to Apple.

Skills	Story Title: CUE HVPA
set up sites	I set up fifteen sites around the state for members to come get their computers and training.
designed training **collaborated**	I designed basic training on setup and operations of the computers and collaborated with Apple trainers to carry it out.
enticed new members	In two months, at zero cost to CUE, I enticed over 5,000 new members to join CUE.
collected $400,000	I collected $150,000 in revenue in dues and $250,000 on the "float."
learned	I learned that you make more money by managing it ("float") than you do by earning it (dues).

Part 2: Trio-ing

Read your story to the other two members in your group of three. As they listen, they jot down the skills they heard in your story and where they heard you use them. They may interrupt you if they need more time to write or further clarification of what you did.

Tell the other members of your trio what skills *you* heard in your own story. When you've finished, let the other two tell you any *additional* skills they heard or any that they found particularly impressive. (I added the *impressive* part. I think we need all the confirmation we can get!) Jot their comments down next to yours in the skills column.

Take turns repeating this process as you hear the stories from the other members of the trio.

Part 3: Prioritizing the skills

After writing seven stories, you will find that certain skills keep popping up in (almost) every story. Dick has a series of activities—you definitely want to buy his book and workbook and go through the whole process—to prioritize the skills you most *enjoyed* using. I learned with the "CUE HVPA" story that although I was able to generate a long list of things I *could* do well, the only one I would ever *like* to do again was— you guessed it!—get more "float" money!

Subsequent stories unearthed dozens of additional skills that I do enjoy and that became the foundation for the career that I customized for myself by the end of the workshop: "stand-up comic, singing priest." (As I said, you need to buy the book and go through the whole process. You may just surprise yourself.)

Activity 10.6

If you are reading this book independently, definitely try writing the stories. Find a friend or two to give you feedback. Everyone involved will be enriched by the process. Even if you love the career you are in, this can reinforce your commitment and clarify your sense of direction.

In a class or workshop, you could have participants in trios write one short story (limit to one page) to get a taste of the process. They could continue to write the other six stories on their own. Unless, of course, your topic is "Career-Life-Mission-Planning," in which case you would have Dick's *Parachute* materials and commit the time to have your students or audience members write and share all seven stories.

And who knows? You, too, could be a budding stand-up performer. God only knows that the world could use more comedic priests. Father Guido Sarducci and I would love to have you join us!

In your past, and that of your students and audiences—besides the heap of known and hitherto undiscovered talents—there may also be lingering another kind of story. One that left wounds or regrets that optimally could have, should have had a different ending. Depending how you wish to deal with this issue, you can take a quick and light-hearted or a longer, deeper view of "re-righting" the past.

Activity 10.7

Identify an episode that might have had a happier ending and work to rewrite (to make right) that ending. A few lighthearted candidates for "righting" might include

- Last week's football or soccer game
- Your score on a recent pop quiz
- Your falling off the diet wagon

Don't like the past? Right it as you rewrite it. Take only from the past what is resourceful for the present and the future.

Think of that great example in the punctuation book that transforms the violent *Eats, Shoots and Leaves* to the gentler *Eats Shoots and Leaves*.[16]

Invite others to experience (see, hear, smell, touch, taste) with you only the commas you need to carry forward. Delete the rest.

Another transformative mentor and friend, Jim Brazell, takes a radically different approach. In fact, his company is even called *The Radical Platypus!*[17]

The Radical Platypus

Multiple perspectives
on innovation and learning:

- Storytelling artist
- Playful scientist
- STEM-arts integrator
- Cyber teacher
- Socratic engineer
- Social technologist
- Presentations velcrologist

lisa@radicalplatypus.com
(210) 555-3443

Jim never talks about the past. His presentations have a decidedly future orientation. And his workshops—or *PlayShops* as he and co-presenter Bob Allen[18] call them—are all about creating "future stories":

> The source of innovation in all of us is storytelling. It is what differentiates us from the rest of the animal kingdom. Our ability to tell stories—fiction and nonfiction—is at the root of our survival, adaptation, and existence. When stories are about what is [to be] done next, they are more than powerful; they are transformative.[19]

In one of Jim and Bob's PlayShops that I was privileged to attend, teachers and administrators worked in teams to position themselves ten years in the future and use the 2020 perspective to look back on 2010 with 2020 vision. Creative juices were flying and participants amazed (and applauded) themselves when they shared solutions they never would have imagined had they kept the focus on the current state of affairs. Jim always makes a video of the event as a memento for the client. Have a look if you want to see the enthusiasm![20]

The small group I was working with focused on the challenge that teachers (who feel like dinosaurs) face trying to keep up with the technology that students take for granted. We decided to illustrate our future story with characters we had carved out of Play-Doh. Ironic that better solutions for technology challenges came from playing with Play-Doh than from staring at a blank computer screen. (Reminds me of the story about Einstein when he confesses that the theory of relativity came to him as he was daydreaming; only afterward did he back into the mathematical formulas.)

The teachers in our story ended up with iPads . . .

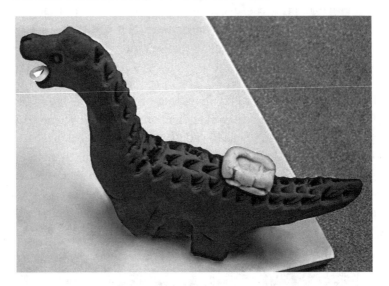

. . . and our students soared like eagles.

Bob mentioned the amazing neural connections between the fingers and the brain. But he and Jim didn't just *talk* about it. They made sure we all *experienced* it! When we walked into the room, every table was *equipped* (notice, I didn't say *decorated*) not only with several kinds of Play-Doh, but also with colored marking pens, glitter pens (who knew?), colored blocks, small squeezable toys, many-colored sticky notes, scissors, glue, colored papers, pipe cleaners, various colored writing pads, crazy-shaped pens and pencils, grid paper, glass beads, and brightly wrapped candies. Jim and Bob never had to *say*, "Today, we're going to have fun." They *showed* us from the moment we walked into the room! And—I know this is a radical notion, but—the presenters did not ask us to refrain from touching anything on the table until they could demonstrate how to use it!

Activity 10.8

In your next class session or workshop, have participants create a future story as a solution to some current problem. Move the initial production phase from "hands-on" computers to "fingers-on" play-inducing-objects.

Warning: Do not do this unless you want creativity to ensue.

In her digital storytelling workshops, Bernajean Porter reminds participants: "Storytelling is not just five slides with some copyright-free music. It's about deciding that you want to fly so much that you are willing to give up being a caterpillar. It's about changing the world into the story you want to see."[21] You can start, suggests Bernajean, by making a new story of your day and taking that to bed with you. (It doesn't cost any more to celebrate than it does to disparage.)

Your students, your audiences are coming to you and saying, "You hasta tell me a story." Whether you tap into lessons from the past or mine the future for creative solutions, don't settle for an inappropriate gray dog or the frou-frou of rented frosting. Go for the stories with substance. Stories can inspire personal transformation and the creation of a better world. They are the only thing that can.

Engaging senses

You've heard the expression: "Stop and smell the roses." Maybe you've even done a reasonable job of mastering the concept. Weather permitting, you've taken the time to walk on scenic trails and to lie in the warm sand on your favorite beach. And you never take a rainbow for granted.

But what if you interpreted the expression literally? Instead of taking the *time* to smell the roses, what if you focused on actually *smelling* them? On *touching* the velvety-soft petals and *seeing* the contrast between the creamy-white blossom and the dark-green stem?

Activity 11.1

Make a list of all the senses you could use to experience the rose.

If you are in a class, break out into groups of three and take turns passing the rose—real or imagined—around the group. (Doing this activity with a real, fresh-cut rose creates an unforgettable experience.) Have each person add one more sense for as long as it, ahem, makes sense. Give each person at least three chances to put in his or her two cents worth. To stoke the fires of your imagination, to see the rose with new eyes, try playing various dramatic roles, for example, curious child, ardent lover, exotic dancer, and so on. As always, positive humor and playful whimsy are encouraged. See if you can come up with at least ten senses on your own or pick your ten favorites from Google's list of over eight hundred million.

How can we put all these senses into play in our classrooms and other presentation venues? To find out, put on some relaxing music, brew yourself a cup of soothing tea, light an aromatic candle, and let's begin our multisensory adventure!

Vision and hearing

Our first stop is plain to see. All my presentations since 1995 have used full-screen, full-color photographic images. Especially during the critical opening moments of a class or presentation—that hallowed time when the most minds are still paying attention—we want to engage the visual sense by displaying a compelling image that subsequent discussions can reference. What are we presenting? What memorable image could best kick off that presentation topic? For example, take cell phones—anything from cell-phone-usage policy to the potential of harnessing cell phones for instruction.

A good place to start would be with an anchor image like this one (taken at the Georgia Aquarium's penguin exhibit in Atlanta) depicting the ubiquity of cell phones. The picture will make people smile—a good way to start any lesson or presentation—and you'll have already epitomized the opportunity: All the kids have cell phones, so what are we going to do with them?

Activity 11.2

Let's try this with another image. Brainstorm what topic(s) the following image (taken at the Botanical Gardens in Atlanta) might serve to anchor.

If you are in a class, break out into groups of three to discuss and then share your best ideas with the large group.

Sometimes the anchor image can actually be a rapid-fire *series* of images, as demonstrated by my niece's autobiographical presentation titled "The Six Sides of Shanta," simulated here as a HyperStudio slideshow. As the cube rotates to each picture, Shanta does a live, voice-over narration to introduce herself to her classmates.

1. Hi, my name is Shanta.
2. I love to hang out with my friends.

3. I'm enjoying the independence of college life . . .

4. . . . although spiders still totally freak me out.

5. I continue to work for world peace.

6. And, oh yeah, I won the bubble-gum-blowing contest in my dorm.

Activity 11.3

Think of topics you are teaching or presenting in which a quick spin of the six-sided cube could serve to introduce and anchor new material.

In the single-image examples of the cell phone and the frog kissing, as well as the spinning cube examples of Shanta, the presenter engages our *vision* with full-screen pictures and our *hearing* with informative, voice-over narration. Two senses are used; and the visual channel (busy processing the images) is not overloaded by redundant on-screen text competing for attention. This models the research-based recommendations that Richard E. Mayer details in his *Multimedia Learning*.[1] In this widely cited book, Mayer shares both the research assumptions behind his research[2]—

Assumption	Description	Supporting Research
Dual channels	Humans possess separate channels for processing **visual** and **auditory** information.	Paivio, 1986[3] Baddeley, 1997[4]
Limited capacity	Humans are limited in the amount of information that they can process in each channel at one time.	Baddeley, 1997 Chandler and Sweller, 1991[5]

—and his comparisons of methods to implement various features of multimedia presentations.[6]

Feature	Traditional Method	More Effective Method
Multimedia[7]	Words alone (single-medium method)	Words and **pictures** (multimedia method)
Modality[8]	Graphics and printed text (text method)	Graphics and **narration** (narration method)
Redundancy[9]	Animation, narration, and on-screen text (redundant method)	Animation and narration (nonredundant method)

Shanta—who could be a poster child for Mayer—got us to look. She got us to listen. But, like Mayer—and most researchers, writers, and performers on the presentation circuit—she limited her presentation strategies to these two senses. The "multimedia" is still just sit-and-get, that is, *sit* and look at my images; listen and *get* my words. But how long can an audience sit? How long can students listen? (It turns out not more than ten minutes.[10]) So, unless your presentation is mercifully brief or your class period is extremely short, you need some additional strategies. You need to move beyond Mayer's multi*media* world ("discovering productive ways of adding pictures to words"[11]) to the even more engaging world of multi*sensory* learning experiences.

Smell

The first stop on *that* journey is as obvious as the nose on your face: your sense of smell.

Activity 11.4

Divide the audience or class members into two groups and seat them at opposite ends of the room. On the wall next to one group (or on the wrists of several volunteers), spray a pleasant-smelling perfume (just enough so they can smell it but the other group can't). I recommend Chocolovers[12] unless you have another perfume that you particularly enjoy.

Chocolovers™ by Aquolina Perfume for Women

Chocolate for the body, mind and soul. Not just a metaphor for sensuality, the scent of chocolate has incredible powers.

The intense but delicate notes of Chocolovers will fill you with energy and serenity every moment of the day.

Have everyone close his or her eyes while you (the teacher-presenter) read a short passage on the health benefits of dark chocolate.[13]

Now spray the other wall (and wrists of volunteers in the second group) plus a few reinforcing sprays to the first group.

Administer a short quiz.[14]

Which group performed better?

Lest you conclude that, well, obviously, everything goes better with chocolate, John Medina conducted a similar experiment in his molecular biology classes at the University of Washington using Brut rather than Chocolovers. He still found that students exposed to the perfume *during learning* did better on the test—sometimes dramatically better—than those who were not.[15]

Medina shared another experiment in which two groups of people munched on popcorn as they watched a movie together. Then they reported to the lab for a memory test. While the control group took the test under normal (without the popcorn smell) conditions, the experimental group was led into a room with the smell of popcorn wafting into the air. In the presence of the popcorn smell, those participants remembered up to 50 percent more information from the movie![16]

Are you thinking what I'm thinking? Classroom teachers, why not serve small bags of popcorn to each student as you are reviewing for a test and then a second bag during the test? Presenters, why not give participants a small bag of popcorn as they come into your session and as they leave a second bag to share with a friend or colleague as they recount what they learned during your wonderful presentation?

Presentations consultant Kare Anderson suggests lightly scenting handouts to further increase attendee recall.[17] For a meeting with a beach theme, she recommends coconut-perfumed suntan lotion. (To accommodate persons with allergies to perfumes, perhaps attendees could choose from a scented or unscented pile.)

Activity 11.5

Think of a conference or presentation theme or a topic you might teach that you could associate with a particular (preferably) pleasant smell.

How would you propel the smell?

All these formal and informal experiments illustrate something scientists have known for years: Smell can evoke memory. It's called the Proust effect, after French author Marcel Proust's most famous recollection when a small, cookie-like pastry enabled him to experience the past as a simultaneous part of his present:

> And suddenly the memory revealed itself: The taste was that of the little piece of madeleine which on Sunday mornings at Combray . . . when I went to say good morning to [my aunt Léonie], [she] used to give me, dipping it first in her own cup of tea.[18]

Have *you* ever been struck by a smell that could take you back in time and place? In the global research study that branding guru Martin Lindstrom undertook for his latest book, *BRAND Sense*, an astounding 90 percent of women and 80 percent of men reported that *smell* frequently formed memory associations from their past.[19] The idea has not been lost on American businesses. When a branch of Barclay's bank started brewing fresh coffee in the mornings, patronage increased by 12 percent.[20] Another study showed the smell of fresh oranges reduces anxiety, promotes serenity, and fosters positive moods among patients waiting in a dentist's office.[21]

Activity 11.6

Stand up. Find someone you don't know. Walk over to that person and take turns sharing something you just learned about the power of smell.

Discuss at what point you might infuse the smell of coffee or oranges into your next presentation or classroom unit.

Taste

Taste is probably the most underused of the senses in presentations and the teaching-learning environment. In preschool and early elementary grades, teachers may introduce children to the major tastes the tongue can sense by having them savor samples of bitter lemons, sweet candy, salty potato chips, and bitter unsweetened cocoa. Teachers may also celebrate ethnic diversity by having students (or their parents) bring in delicacies representing the cuisine of different cultural groups or particular countries they happen to be studying. Then there was the annual proposal-reading workshop I gave for many years at the Alameda County Office of Education in Hayward, California. My father baked his inimitable cookies for the participants and people would come year after year for the cookies. I never measured whether it increased learning but it definitely helped attendance. Dad filled the room every year!

Activity 11.7

Have you experienced instances when something tasty actually enhanced the learning experience? Brainstorm presentation venues when learning could involve taste. Recognize that smell will also be part of the experience. (As *BRAND Sense* author Martin Lindstrom shares: "It's possible to leverage aroma without including taste. However, taste without smell is virtually impossible."[22])

Bodily-kinesthetic senses

Teachers around the country are finding that students learn better when they add movement to the lessons. Eeva Reeder, former math teacher in the Mountlake Terrace School District just north of Seattle, Washington, took her students out on the concrete playground and had them plot themselves as points on a graph. She shares: "There's a memory in the body. In ten minutes, my students learned more about the fundamental nature of lines and parabolas than they would in a month of just bookwork. My advice to other teachers? Try it. It has an impact."[23]

Activity 11.8

Stand up and find five people you hardly know. Bunch yourselves close together and move almost imperceptibly. Think of your group as a solid mass.

Next, disperse a bit and move around gracefully, with fluid gestures. Think of your group as a liquid underwater ballet troupe.

Finally, spread way out, run, and jump around like crazy. Forget your other group members and just have a gas. Maybe bump into some people from other groups. Definitely burst into laughter if and when you do!

Sure, science teachers could use this activity to teach states of matter. But what about workshop presenters using the activity to infuse some energy into the audience? And then applying the concept metaphorically to something like how best to move toward *change* in the organization?

Sometimes, as professors or presenters we have hundreds of people crammed into a theater with fixed seating and there's very little room to move around. In these situations, instead of sitting down and entering answers to multiple-choice questions on audience response systems (clickers), why not have the participants stand up and "vote" with their bodies?

Activity 11.9

Let's see who's in the audience (or class) today!

If you're working (or plan to be working) . . .

- In administration, face the front of the room
- In higher ed, turn and face the right-hand wall
- At the elementary school, face the left-hand wall
- At the high school, face the back wall
- At the middle school, sit down (and conserve your energy)

Give yourselves a round of applause and thank you all for coming today!

Discovery Education evangelist Hall Davidson shared that he was recently conducting a workshop in which he wanted to poll a group of superintendents but the clickers weren't working. Hall's quick thinking saved the day: he had the superintendents—good-humored folks every one—line up into a human bar graph and look around the room to see which line was longest!

You don't get to be a school superintendent without a well-developed humor gene. I remember attending a workshop in which seven or eight district administrators had spelled out a word using their bodies to form the letters. At the far-right end of the word, their six-foot, two-inch superintendent jumped straight up into the air—to represent the exclamation point! (I don't remember the word, but I'll never forget James Smith's punctuation!)

Activity 11.10

If you can move the chairs (or have space up front) in a presentation venue, try the body-spelling activity. Divide into groups of four. Think of a four-letter word you can demonstrate that would teach a particularly interesting orthographical phenomenon.

For example, you could pick a word like *knit*, where the bodies would shape and sound out the last three letters and then—pause—watch the "silent *k*" slip stealthily into place.

Or choose a word like *hear*, where you put the beginning and ending consonants in place, and then have two vowels (hand-in-hand) go walking, and the first one does the talking. (The second vowel puts its finger over its lips.)

Depending on the size of the group and the time allocated for this activity, you may have all the groups or just three or four groups volunteer to body-spell their word.

Those of you who are working in classrooms in which the weekly spelling list is still a requirement, try moving all the desks to the perimeter of the classroom (a little serendipitous math lesson) and have the students body-spell the words. Group students according to the length of the words and let teams choose a word from the list. See if the other groups can decipher it. Or have four to six teams and see which team can body-spell the word first. Can anyone spell *fun*? How about *pandemonium*? It may take a little experimentation to get the right balance of physicality and pedagogy but somewhere along the way the abstract rules will start to make sense and, instead of dreading the list, the kids will start asking, "When can we do spelling?"

Touch

Today, with valid concerns, many schools are advising teachers to make no physical contact whatsoever with students. I would agree with *Multisensory Learning* author Lawrence Baines: "There is nothing inappropriate about a pat on the back for a job well done or a nudge on the arm as an indication that 'I want you to succeed.'"[24] And for presentations to adults, the handshake is still a socially acceptable way of satisfying that basic human need for physical contact.

Although that person-to-person aspect of touch is limited by social conventions, the use of touch for gathering information is limited only by issues of safety, budget, and—in the end—our imagination. Who can forget the classic blindfold tests (most often executed on dark and scary nights such as Halloween) in which you ran your fingers over—eek!—eyeballs before you realized those were just the olives your mom bought that afternoon at the delicatessen.

And, taking off the blindfold, what about this photo of my Caribbean vacation? Yes, that's me swimming with the stingray (and the smiling tour guide).

Nice photo, but how much more real, rich, and memorable could I make it by having my audiences *feel* pieces of sandpaper—rough . . . like the back of the stingray—and little cups of custard—smooth . . . like the stingray's silky underbelly?

Combining touch with visual information, research tells us, increases recognition-learning by almost 30 percent compared with either one alone.[25]

A wonderful project called *Image-Making Within the Writing Process*[26] put this research into practice by providing sheets of textured paper for children to tear, paint, and glue into collages to stimulate more creative writing.

This collage—with its rosy pink clouds swirling above the turquoise blue and purple waters and the stunning yellow boat—inspired a first-grader to write: "And the clouds in the sky were like fluffy pink pancakes." And, quite proud of herself, to announce: "I can't believe a first-grader wrote that!"

Multiple senses

It's no secret that early elementary teachers consider manipulative materials a godsend for reinforcing basic math concepts. But Louise Fiori teaches seventh grade! Fiori and several other teachers featured in a special issue of *Instructor* magazine[27] on multiple intelligences have applied Howard Gardner's theory and have done an amazing job of harnessing children's different gifts for learning. In doing so, they have naturally engaged multiple *senses* as well as multiple intelligences.

While pulling apart a tangerine, this middle-school student

- *Feels* the segments as she
- *Sees* them coming from the whole tangerine, and she
- *Smells* the fresh orange scent as she literally
- *Tastes* the fruit (what else were you going to do with it?) and
- *Hears* her teacher give directions for the activity.

During the next few days and weeks as the teacher complements this hands-on experience with other concrete examples of fractions and eventually more abstract applications of the concept, she can evoke the tangerine-segmenting activity by passing around another fresh tangerine. And—similar to Marcel Proust with his little madeleine— the children will relive the *past* experience simultaneously with its *present* application.

In other words, although using multisensory, concrete methodology such as the tangerine-segmenting activity is *not* the be-all and end-all of teaching fractions, it *is* the begin-all. Introducing a new concept to students (or audiences) of any age in abstract terms reminds me of this uncannily astute student evaluation of a Stanford professor: "He would write stuff on the board until *he* understood. Then he would sit down."

Of course, we want the professor, the K–12 teacher, the presenter at your district in-service or the keynoter at your professional organization's annual conference to "know his stuff" at the abstract level. We recognize that most of them did, at some point, have to write a doctoral thesis with abstract words rather than concrete blocks but we would hope that somewhere along the way they took a French class. Read a little Proust. Sniffed and savored a tangerine or two . . .

So, now, with our senses heightened, let's go back to "The Six Sides of Shanta" presentation. Plotting the engaged senses on Lindstrom's pentagonal *Sensogram*,[28] we can see clearly that with her full-screen images and voice-over narration, Shanta tapped the senses of vision and hearing.

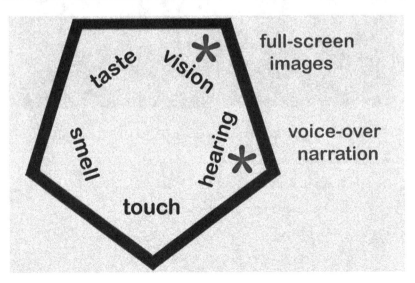

How could Shanta tap into other senses to make her presentation more memorable? Maybe a piece of bubble gum (taste, smell) for everyone in the class to go with the bubble gum-blowing picture? Or possibly a small peace charm to examine (vision, touch) as she shows the slide of her giving the peace sign? Or having some of her friends come in and shake hands (touch) when she shows the slide of her friends? Perhaps a bag of rubber spiders (touch) from the Dollar Store tossed into the crowd? Or not. Knowing that 75 percent of emotional response is based on what people smell,[29] what about Shanta's replacing one of her slides with an image related to a favorite fragrance such as fresh-cut lemons[30] that she could pass around to smell?

Or, better yet, finding a yummy lemon meringue pie to taste?

Think about translating the research about multimedia learning and multisensory branding into your presentation practice. Start including more sensory dimensions and see your effectiveness soar by up to 300 percent.[31]

When you brainstormed earlier about smelling the rose, after the five basic physiological senses—vision, hearing, smell, touch, and taste—what were the other senses you tapped into? Although it goes beyond the purview of this book, I would hope that a "sense of purpose" figured high on your list. Knowing *why* we live gives direction for what to pursue and the power to go about achieving it.

PART 3

Resolution

res•o•lu•tion |ˌrezəˈloōSHən|

noun

1 pixel dimensions, the number of pixels displayed in each dimension: WXGA resolution is 1280 pixels wide by 800 high.

2 solution to a challenge or problem: She offered resolutions for common presentation pitfalls.

3 a decision to do something or to behave in a certain manner: He always wrote down his New Year's resolutions.

In this final chapter we'll review ten of the easiest-to-implement strategies for avoiding common presentation pitfalls.

We'll have coffee and donuts and change caterpillars into butterflies. The first part is my treat; the last, your challenge.

Putting it all together

Of all the presentations I've given lately, my favorite is titled "Ten Shots to Caffeinate Your Presentations." It's my best attempt at giving audience members as many practical tips as possible without overwhelming the already overloaded folks who show up for the session. I know that administrators who have survived layoffs are now doing their original jobs plus the work of colleagues who have been reassigned or retired. Classroom teachers are trying to prepare students for high-stakes tests and still find time for projects and activities that engage students in real learning. College professors and other professional presenters are working furiously to keep up with the latest technology, deliver meaningful content, *and* find ways to boost enrollment and garner *standing* rather than *walking* ovations. And students, as always, are trying to get through their courses (and we hope learning something along the way) and still have time for a life. For all these constituents as well as the parents, board members, industry representatives, consultants, and other wonderful people who attend my presentations, I feel obligated to make sure their time is well spent, that they leave with something they didn't know before they came in, and with the strategies, tools, resources, and confidence to put their new knowledge to practical use in ways that will make both their work and personal lives more meaningful and effective.

For those of you reading this book, I feel that same kind of obligation. In the first eleven chapters I've handed you a thousand puzzle pieces that may take a while to put together. So, how can I help you find just the right pieces for the lesson you need to teach tomorrow morning? Or the presentation you're scheduled to give on Friday? And how can we make it creative and fun—not like one of those wooden puzzles with rigid indentations where each piece can only fit in one place, but more like a Silly Putty puzzle where hands get dirty mashing up wads and globs and rolling giggles and glitter into the mix! Oh, yes, and how can we do this with time we can't find and money we don't have?

Perhaps the most efficient way to proceed, before the ink dries on these pages, would be for us to continue working on the puzzle, have a nice cup of coffee together, and recap ten of the most potent "shots" that I would recommend to caffeinate your next presentation. My treat.

1. Tweak the text

I'd like to say, "*lose* the text," as in "no text on your slides—zero, zip, nada," but I know that's like tearing the net out from under an already scary trapeze act. So, until you're comfortable, let's try three interim approaches:

1. Less text (smaller net)
2. Well-formatted text (smaller and better net)
3. No text (no net but with a shorter act)

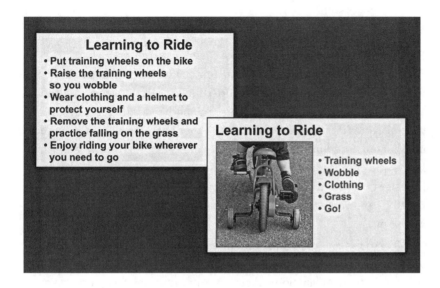

Less text

Remember the example from Nancy Duarte's *slide:ology* (in Chapter Seven) in which she took the typical text-laden slide, reduced the text in each bullet point to one or two key words, and then replaced those words with a picture?[1]

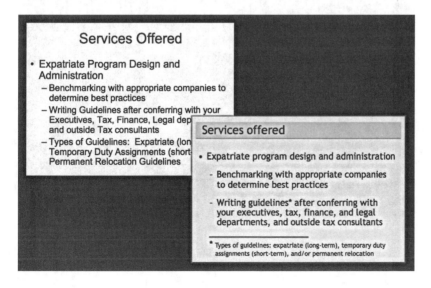

Well-formatted text

Recall the before-and-after views of Dave's résumé we looked at in Chapter One. If you are going to use text, never display more than six words across or six lines down. More than six words across and the audience blinks, loses its place, and can't bother finding it again. More than six lines down and the audience tunes out, overwhelmed by the anticipated boredom. Compare any of your text slides to Dave's. See how lowercase is faster to read than uppercase, how left-justified text is easier to follow than centered, how varied leading (space between the lines) organizes information better than uniform line spacing, and so on.

Note to instructors and presenters: If you are having your students or audience members work through the transformation of Dave's résumé, instead of *you* pointing out the changes, let *them* work in small groups to spot the improvements. I was amazed the last time I showed Dave in a presentation that the educators in the audience not only identified every change I could have lectured about but also spotted one change I hadn't even noticed!

No text

Who could forget the three-slide sequence where little Johnny introduced his bird (the robin red breast), showed what it ate (Yuck! Worms!), and then revealed its unique (pause for effect . . .) blue eggs! (See Chapter Three.)

With only three slides, and having researched the material himself, Johnny's only need for text was to identify himself and the bird on the first slide.

If you are the typical PowerPoint-wielding adult, you will probably feel most comfortable using a combination of these approaches. If you are a classroom teacher, please do not even offer your PowerPoint newbie students the first two options. Instead of having to wean them later, just train them on the images method from the beginning. With image-only slides, the key—for you as for our second-graders—is to start with a small number of slides (because it takes time to find all those images). For you, think in three- to six-slide modules. Over time, like stringing pearls, you'll end up with the whole, contiguously beautiful necklace.

2. Start with the concrete

There is a continuum between the abstract and the concrete. Take the rose, for example. If you were presenting the concept to an audience that had never seen (or smelled or touched) a rose before, consider the following five approaches (from the most abstract to the most concrete) of introducing the flower in your slideshow:

1. Project the word *rose*

2. Display a clipart rose

3. Fill the screen with a full-color photographic image of a rose

4. Show the video of a rose maybe with "Lo, How a Rose E'er Blooming" playing in the background

5. Hand everyone a real rose!

With time and budget constraints, we may not have the perfect video and long-stemmed roses for every concept in every presentation but at least we can start using more full-screen photographic images.

First the (concrete) image, then the (abstract) words. Remember show-and-tell. There's a reason it's not called *tell-and-show*.

Speaking of show-and-tell, those of you who have attended one of my presentations know that everybody's favorite activity is the Progressive Story, described in Chapter Ten. Participants get into groups of three and each group gets a small, inexpensive Koosh ball[2] to toss around without hurting anybody. The person with the shortest hair starts the story by saying something related to the picture on the first slide, lobs the ball to someone else in the group to continue with the second slide, and so on. It's a great way to introduce new material as well as review and test material you've already covered. Think about using this technique whenever you want to increase the energy level in the room and get everybody participating.

3. Make a handout

Like the cowboy and the horse, the handout and the slide each have a job to do and the jobs are not interchangeable. Images go on the screen (where color is free); text—facts, quotes, references (especially those pesky Internet URLs)—goes on the handout, which is also posted on the Internet for future reference and with links to additional resources. For examples of handouts, refer back to Chapter Two and also help yourself to templates on the DVD provided with this book.

4. Change it up

Just two words to remember here: *ten* and *two*.

- After *ten* minutes of sit and get, audiences need
- A change of pace for at least *two* minutes.

The two minutes is not an unrelated time-out but rather a different way of recapping what was just shared or previewing the coming attraction. It's the perfect time for audience engagement, for connecting with prior knowledge, and for using different modalities to match the learning styles of diverse learners. For more on pacing your presentation, see Chapters Three and Five.

This might be a good time for *you* to stand up, grab your smart phone, and share something you didn't know ten minutes ago! (Please keep calls on topic and under two minutes. Please keep text messages under one hundred-twenty characters. It's good practice. Being succinct and pithy is a much-appreciated skill in today's society. Looks good on your résumé.)

5. Play music

Using music in a presentation is almost too easy. Humans are fundamentally wired for music. (See Chapter Eight.) Incoming music connects to thirty-nine places in the brain and travels on the vagus (some say *Vegas*) nerve to nourish every organ in the body, except the spleen. (That might explain why so many poets used to complain about spleen.)

Music sets the mood instantaneously. Got thirty seconds for a million-dollar Super Bowl commercial? You'd better use music. No time to waste. Music can soothe, energize, inspire—you pick the emotion; it will oblige. (And so will we with royalty-free samples on the DVD. Don't miss that resource!)

6. Follow your passion

What one thing makes you love getting up and going to work or school in the morning? Pause and reflect. Feel the gratitude. It's a healing emotion.

Are you making presentations related to that topic? Are you using skills that you love to convey your message to others? Often, in my presentations, I share the video of the middle school student's musical book report about the Holocaust discussed in Chapter Eight. The emotional topic was made all the more poignant because the student wrote and sang a song about the situation. People cry when I show that video. They know for sure that she understood the message of the books.

It's the passion that connects, that passes the torch. Look at what you have to present and find something in it that you love. Sometimes it's a stretch. Sometimes you have to go through the motions and the love will follow. Worst case, as these rock lyrics suggest, "If you can't be with the one you love, love the one you're with."

7. Create a context

We know from Robert Marzano's research that identifying similarities and differences is the, bar none, most effective teaching strategy![3] And we know from our own intuition and experience plus the research from John Medina that "[v]ision trumps all the other senses."[4] So why not marry the two and juxtapose *images* to make comparisons?

Now, comparisons work best if you can see both images at the same time. With the new, wider LCD projectors (shaped like HDTV screens), the presenter has room to put images side by side on the same slide. The second image can come in as a build (once the first image has been studied) or the two images can be presented together for the audience to start making the comparison.

Imagine, for example, a presentation on the seasons in which you juxtapose a golden maple leaf and a golden daffodil on the same slide.

Alternatively, you could display a portion of one wide image and then use the slideshow's wipe-right or wipe-left transition to reveal the rest of that single image. (I like to show the cartoon of a farmer gloating over the life-sized, plump, and frumpy female scarecrow he has just plunked down in his garden. Then I wipe right to reveal his wife—who looks exactly like the scarecrow—saying "Not funny.")

Of course, on a more serious note, great orators can also create comparisons with their *word* pictures. Think of Martin Luther King Jr.'s famous "I Have a Dream" speech when he verbally painted a series of contrasts between what was and what could be. In sixteen minutes, he was interrupted by applause twenty-seven times! If the contrast is clear, the choice is clear as well.

8. Infuse humor

Humor is also about juxtapositions. When people in the audience burst into laughter, it means they have juxtaposed your new content with their prior knowledge. It's *their* laughter that makes *your* information stick. In other words, if you can make them laugh, you can make them learn!

The more serious you are about your content, the more essential it is that you deliver and reinforce it with humor. Get in the habit of taking your camera everywhere you go. You never know when life will offer you the perfect image for your next presentation, such as the following one of Tacoma, Washington, middle school teacher Stacie Jensen.

It's time for a short "stretch break." Please stand up and see if you can match Stacie's flexibility.

Or, at least, laugh trying!

9. Engage emotions

Emotions are at the heart of what we do as educators. As you may recall from Chapter Nine, we discussed tapping emotions in at least three ways:

1. *Create a positive ambiance for learning.* Whether or not you are conscious of it, your emotions set the stage for what you teach or present. Whatever you are "thinking" in your heart radiates at least fifteen feet in every direction.[5] As a presenter or workshop leader, you can wander around the conference room before your presentation starts. By just thinking positive thoughts as you chitchat with folks, you can change the mood of the group and create a positive atmosphere in the room. You do not have to announce what you are doing because it works on an autonomic level, without the conscious acquiescence of the audience. However, depending on the situation and your relationship with the group, you may choose to do so:

   - For example, at the end of a day-long workshop when I have clearly bonded with the participants, I might ask them: "Were there any indications that I was excited to work with you today? How did that make you feel?"

   - My dear friend Cathy Baumgartner decided to be even more explicit. After hearing my explanation of the HeartMath research on emotional synchronization, she borrowed my PowerPoint slides and went back and shared the information with her alternative education high-school students. One of the kids responded by saying, "We know, Mrs. BeeGee. We love you, too!"

2. *Judiciously apply Krazy Glue.* It has been said that emotions are like sticky notes (see Chapter Nine). On further reflection, I would say that presenting your content with great emotion is more like coating it with Krazy Glue. So, do be careful when using emotion. Apply it purposefully and judiciously. (Of the

28,500 articles on Google on how to remove Krazy Glue, most are not pretty and promise only partial success.) And definitely stick to the positive emotions. Our kids get enough of the negative ones outside the classroom.

The emotion-infused stories can be ones you create (such as personal anecdotes) or they can be selections from current or historical events. The most salient example for me is the story of Sacagawea from the Lewis and Clark expedition. As a teacher or presenter, you could lay out the well-documented steps of that 1804–1806 journey from Missouri to the Pacific Coast. Or you could show a video clip of that pivotal moment in the expedition when Sacagawea went to translate at the guns-for-horses negotiations between Captain Lewis and the Shoshone chief.[6]

Another example could be using an emotion-packed video in math class. Say you have to teach ratios. (Be still my beating heart.) Instead of starting with definitions of the abstract concept, try showing the SchoolTube video[7] called "Bad Dates" (described in Chapter Five) in which a young lady just wants "to find a guy who can speak to her on a one-to-one ratio."

3. *Expand understanding of positive emotions.* Remember my suggestion in Chapter Nine that you create an emotional photo wall? Posting photographs—images for words like love, kindness, and gratitude—can change the whole atmosphere of a school. A few posters at the district office or in your presentation venues wouldn't hurt either! Inexpensive selections from companies such as Simple Truths[8] can jump-start the collection, which staff and students can enrich by adding their own photographs and captioned explanations.

By the way, positive and negative emotions cannot coexist. As love will drive out fear, so kindness will put an end to bullying. And gratitude? Ever heard of stress? Runs for its life in the face of gratitude. Remember there is no neutral. Everything is a forced choice. Think of the wedding vows: "for better or worse, in sickness or in health. . . ." Seems like a no-brainer to choose the better, healthier options.

10. Tell stories

That reminds me of a story . . .

Did your ears perk up when you read that line? Everybody loves a great story. In fact, we *need* stories to make sense of the world around us to guide us in this great journey we call *life*. Do you think people come to your classes and your presentations because of the information that you share? If what they wanted was facts, they didn't have to drive across town or fly across the country. They could just Google from home in their pajamas. No, the reason they pay you the big bucks for teaching and presenting is that *you* Google from home, in *your* pajamas, and then you have the skill, experience, and insight to organize all that information—or at least a subset of the eighty-three billion relevant hits—and put it into a compelling story.

Let's face it. You've already lost the ADD crowd if you lecture for more than *two* minutes and the rest of the audience if you go on for more than *ten*. And put up a slide full of bulleted text or—even worse— a spreadsheet in typical teeny-tiny type and everybody immediately jumps from ADD to ADOSS (Attention Deficit . . . Oh, Something Shiny!).[9]

But something happens to the listeners the minute you shift into storytelling mode. As we saw in Chapter Ten, mirror neurons kick into high gear and listeners hang on your every word, sometimes even anticipating what you are going to say next! Once you have grabbed their attention, use it well.

First, make sure you tell the story in a language they understand. May I share one last personal story to illustrate this point? I was doing a presentation on "The Power of Visuals in Teaching and Learning" at the Texas Computer Education Association (TCEA)'s annual conference. The room held three-hundred-plus eager educators, and I had prepared a hundred-and-fifty-slide PowerPoint for the ninety-minute presentation. Long (painful) story short, no one from TCEA could get my laptop to talk to the projector. I smiled at the audience and said, "Let's all go to the Exhibit Hall!" No one budged. I proceeded to deliver the most demanding presentation of my life. On the fly, I created pictures in their mind's eye using only *words* (and my best Italian gestures). Not enough time for one-hundred-fifty image captures but probably at least fifty or sixty. From the nodding heads, rapt attention, and frequent bursts of laughter, it was apparent that they were "seeing" what I was "seeing." For the next two days, people were coming up to me saying that it was the best presentation of the conference! Why did it work? Because the audience was my "tribe." I knew which words could recall images in their visual memory bank. We shared the same prior knowledge. (To use a computer metaphor, we had access to the same server.) It was a homogenous group in which, as a computer-using educator, I was a confident, experienced, and comfortable member.

Compare this to a typical Silicon Valley, California, classroom. Thirty-plus students speaking nine different languages from ten different countries. Homeless students who sleep in broken-down cars. Wealthy students whose parents' private jets fly over those cars. Kids whose parents read to them every night. Kids whose parents have never seen a book. What stories do you tell *them*? And how do you deliver those stories? You pull out every tool in your storyteller's handbag:

- You bring your own LCD projector. You have to have images, no matter what the topic. Those images are by far the most efficient way to build a shared knowledge base together as you go along.

- You play music that sets the emotional tone for the story.

- You make them laugh with your nonverbal humor—over-the-top facial expressions, gestures, pratfalls, and so on.

- You keep it short and simple, always stopping short of the point when they would be frustrated by lack of comprehension.

And the content of those stories? Of course that will vary according to the subjects you are assigned to teach and the topics you are invited to present. But inasmuch as possible, always aim for something adaptable, rich enough to contain jewels for everyone and both universal and personally applicable. If you want your presentation to be a call to action, an invitation to change, then tell a story about someone in a similar situation who faced similar obstacles, made the right choice, and "lived happily ever after" (that is, found the reward to be worth the effort). It's less about *your* knowledge than about *their* change of heart.

In the course of this book, I have shared many stories with you to illustrate and organize the best of what I've gleaned from my decades of research and personal experience as an educator. Along the way, I've prodded, teased, cajoled, encouraged, and, I hope, persuaded you to transform the way you design and deliver educational presentations. I know firsthand that what I'm asking you to do requires a serious commitment. Moving from text-based to image-based slides is like changing from a caterpillar to a butterfly. It's not a trivial process. But compare the two. Which one is more beautiful? Plus, think how much easier it will be to fly once you have wings.

Notes

Introduction

1. Nightmare scenario inspired by Rebecca Ganzel, a freelance writer in St. Paul, Minnesota, author of "PowerPointless" and former managing editor of *Presentations Magazine*. For access to the complete article and additional entertaining and informative writing by Rebecca Ganzel and other presentations experts, register with the *Training Magazine* website: www.trainingmag.com.

Chapter 1

1. Edward Tufte (born 1942) is an American statistician and professor emeritus of political science, statistics, and computer science at Yale University. He is noted for his writings on information design and visual literacy, which deal with the visual communication of information. In his 2003 essay, "The Cognitive Style of PowerPoint: Pitching Out Corrupts Within," Tufte criticizes the simplistic thinking and linear progression through an artificial hierarchy engendered by the PowerPoint bulleted templates. The thirty-two-page booklet is available from Amazon.com.

2. Garr Reynolds, author of *Presentation Zen* (Berkeley, CA: New Riders, 2008) and *Presentation Zen Design* (Berkeley, CA: New Riders, 2009), is a former Apple employee (Cupertino), jazz musician, communications specialist, and design evangelist. He is currently associate professor of management at Kansai Gaidai University in Osaka, Japan, where he teaches marketing, global marketing, and multimedia presentation design. Garr is active in the Japanese community and can often be found presenting

on subjects concerning design, branding, and effective corporate communications.

3. Nancy Duarte, author of *slide:ology: The Art and Science of Great Presentations* (Sebastopol, CA: O'Reilly Media, 2008), was responsible for the creation of the slides Al Gore used in the movie *An Inconvenient Truth*. CEO of Duarte Design since 1990, Nancy Duarte passionately pursues the presentation development and design niche. One of the largest design firms in Silicon Valley and listed as a top woman-owned business in the area, Duarte Design is one of the few agencies in the world focused solely on presentations, whether they are delivered in person, online, or via mobile device.

4. Roger Wagner, creator of the groundbreaking *HyperStudio* (1982–1999, 2007–present), private pilot, rare book collector, writer, author, amateur scientist, inventor, with ancillary interests and expertise in music, mathematics, linguistics, science, history, and architecture, maintains that anything worth doing is worth overdoing! Catch one of his spotlight speaker sessions or laugh and learn at his inimitable performances as French computer guru/bartender in Roger's Bistro at the MacKiev booth in the exhibit hall at educational technology conferences from California to Texas to Florida.

5. Chip Heath and Dan Heath, columnists for *Fast Company* magazine and coauthors of the book *Made to Stick: Why Some Ideas Survive and Others Die* (New York: Random House, 2008), which has been a *New York Times*, *Wall Street Journal*, and *BusinessWeek* best seller. Chip's research examines why certain ideas—ranging from urban legends to folk medical cures, from *Chicken Soup for the Soul* stories to business strategy myths—survive and prosper in the social marketplace of ideas. These "naturally sticky" ideas spread without external help in the form of marketing dollars, PR assistance, or the attention of leaders. Dan conducted research for Harvard Business School, where he coauthored ten case studies on entrepreneurial ventures. He subsequently worked for the executive education division of Duke University, where he designed and taught in training programs for Fortune 500 executives.

6. Daniel Pink is the author of four books focused on the changing world of work, including *The New York Times* best seller *A Whole New Mind: Why Right-Brainers Will Rule the Future* (New York:

Penguin, 2006). Pink's articles on business and technology have appeared in *The New York Times, Harvard Business Review, Fast Company,* and *Wired.* Pink also speaks to corporations, associations, universities, and education conferences on topics such as the shift from the Information Age—with its premium on logical, linear, computer-like abilities—to what he calls "the Conceptual Age," when "right-brain" qualities such as empathy, inventiveness, and meaning predominate.

7. Simons, Tad, "PowerPoint Xtreme" seminar, Training/Presentations Conference 2002, Georgia World Congress Center, Atlanta.

8. Medina, John, *Brain Rules: 12 Principles for Surviving and Thriving at Work, Home, and School* (Seattle: Pear Press, 2008), p. 239.

9. Duarte, Nancy, *slide:ology*, p. 116.

10. Ibid., p. 118.

11. Reynolds, Garr, *Presentation Zen*, p. 122.

12. Sanford ArtEdventures, "Color Theory," 1999 [Online article was posted at http://www.sanford-artedventures.com/play/color2/d2a.html].

13. 3M Corporation research cited in "The Power of Color in Presentations," 3M Meeting Network Articles & Advice, 2001 [Online article was posted at http://www.presentations.com/deliver/audience/1998/05/13_fl_psy_01.html].

14. Wagner, Carlton, *Color Power* (Chicago: Wagner Institute for Color Research, 1985), p. 103.

15. Ibid., pp. 103, 110.

16. An excellent reference is the section on "Color" in Nancy Duarte's *slide:ology*, pp. 126–139.

17. According to Wikipedia, the red-green combination affects males much more often than females because the genes for the red and green color receptors are located on the X chromosome, of which males have only one and females have two. [Online article available: http://en.wikipedia.org/wiki/Color_blindness—Red-green_color_blindness].

18. Morton, J. L., *Color and Culture Matters*, 2001 [Online article available: www.colormatters.com/culturematters.html].

19. Tufte, Edward, *Envisioning Information* (Cheshire, CT: Graphics Press,, 1990), p. 81.

20. Duarte, Nancy, *slide:ology*, p. 126.

21. Medina, John, *Brain Rules*, p. 239.

22. This image from Masayoshi Takahashi's presentation is courtesy of Phillip Toland's presentation at www.slideshare.net/philtoland/presentation-zen-1655196.

23. www.slideshare.net/jbrenman/thirst.

24. Duarte, Nancy, *slide:ology*, p. 140.

25. *Kerning* refers to the horizontal space between letters. Typefaces that are tightly kerned (such as Times and Arial) are good for print documents because they save space. Typefaces that are widely kerned (such as Georgia and Verdana) are better for projected presentations because the letters don't collide on the screen.

26. Duarte, Nancy, *slide:ology*, p. 152.

27. Concept borrowed from an Adobe print ad on the importance of typefaces, circa 1995.

Chapter 2

1. Nielson, Jakob, "Top Ten Mistakes in Web Page Design" 1996 [Online article available: http://www.useit.com/alertbox/9605a.html].

2. www.apolloideas.com/thirst.

3. www.youtube.com/watch?v=-oM8os_8QgQ.

4. www.bonniestjohn.com.

5. Medina, John, *Brain Rules*, p. 74.

6. *Redundant:* When the same words from the slides are printed on the handout and read by the presenter

7. *Complementary:* Acting as or providing a complement (something that completes the whole); mutually making up what is lacking; that which completes or brings to perfection

8. *Synergistic:* When the whole is greater than the sum of the individual parts; cooperative, working together, interacting, mutually stimulating

9. Mayer, Richard E., *Multimedia Learning* (2nd ed.) (New York: Cambridge University Press, 2009).

10. Ibid.

11. Medina, John, *Brain Rules*, p. 87.

12. Ibid.

13. Ibid.

14. www.oprah.com/packages/no-phone-zone.html

15. Tolle, Eckhart, *A New Earth: Awakening to Your Life's Purpose* (New York: Penguin Books, 2005), p. 202.

16. Ibid., p. 297.

17. Ibid., p. 301.

18. Ibid., pp. 25–27.

19. www.t2.com/waterbuffalo.

Chapter 3

1. TEDTalks—riveting talks by remarkable people, free to the world; archived at www.ted.com/talks.

2. "Billy Graham: A Man with a Mission Impossible," special section, *Cincinnati Post*, June 27, 2002 [Online article available: www.highbeam.com/doc/1G1–87912863.html].

3. Tolle, Eckhart, *A New Earth*, p. 229.

4. Ibid., p. 230.

5. www.tonyrobbins.com/testimonials.

6. Gallo, Carmine, *The Presentation Secrets of Steve Jobs: How to Be Insanely Great in Front of Any Audience* (New York: McGraw-Hill, 2000).

7. Ibid., p. 197.

8. See the complete list of presentation titles on my website: www.educatebetter.org/presentations.html.

9. For a copy of the form contact Jim directly at Jim.Brazell@ radicalplatypus.com.

10. To make and laminate the posters, see www.variquest.com/ poster-maker-3600 and www.variquest.com/cold-laminators.

11. One of the premier authorities on Howard Gardner's multiple intelligences and their application in education is Dr. Thomas Armstrong. Visit his website for more information: www.thomasarmstrong .com/multiple_intelligences.php.

Chapter 4

1. Ainsworth, Larry, *Power Standards: Identifying the Standards That Matter the Most* (Englewood, CO: Lead + Learn Press, 2003).

2. Marzano, Robert, and Hawstead, Mark W., *Making Standards Useful in the Classroom* (Alexandria, VA: Association for Supervision and Curriculum Development, 2008).

3. Marzano, Robert, "Representing Knowledge Nonlinguistically," *Educational Leadership*, May 2010, p. 86.

4. Read, Katy, "May I Have My Attention, Please?" *AARP Magazine*, July/August 2010, p. 28.

5. Hallowell, Edward M., M.D., *CrazyBusy: Overstretched, Overbooked, and About to Snap! Strategies for Handling Your Fast-Paced Life* (New York: Ballantine Books, 2007).

6. *Portmanteau* is the French word for a large leather suitcase that opens into two hinged compartments. Literally, it means something to "carry [your] coat"; figuratively, it refers to a new word formed by joining two others and combining their meanings:

   - *smog* from *smoke* and *fog*
   - *motel* from *motor* and *hotel*
   - *brunch* from *breakfast* and *lunch*

From *The American Heritage Dictionary of the English Language* (4th ed.) (Boston: Houghton Mifflin, 2009).

7. Bolles, Richard Nelson, *What Color Is Your Parachute? A Practical Manual for Job-Hunters and Career-Changers* (Berkeley, CA: Ten Speed Press, revised annually). Participants come from all over the world to Dick's home near San Francisco for his much-loved five-day workshop on the subject of "Where Do I Go from Here with My Life?" For details see his website: www.jobhuntersbible.com.

Chapter 5

1. http://aces.nmsu.edu/matrix/. The three-minute "Bad Date" animation reviews concepts behind ratio, giving examples. You can download it for the iPod or as a QuickTime movie. You can also download a learner guide for students and a teacher's guide with additional learning activities as PDFs.

2. Heath, Chip, and Heath, Dan, *Made to Stick*, p. 106.

3. Tips from David S. Rose are included in Garr Reynolds's book, *Presentation Zen Design*, pp. 56–57.

4. Heath, Chip, and Heath, Dan, ibid., p. 104.

5. Rose, ibid., p. 56.

6. www.cloudappreciationsociety.org/gallery/index.php?x= browse&category=20&pagenum=1.

7. In the *Cinderella* fairy tale, the fairy godmother turned two rats into white horses to pull the carriage that delivered Cinderella to the ball.

8. Vikings raiding and trading (787–1066); Crusades (1095–1291); Columbus sailed the ocean blue in 1492; Lewis and Clark (May 1804–September 1806)

9. Medina, John, *Brain Rules*, p. 81.

10. Ibid., p. 75.

11. Ibid.

12. Read the entire April 8, 2007, article "Pearls Before Breakfast," by *Washington Post* staff writers Emily Shroder, Rachel Manteuffel, John W. Poole, and Tom Shroder or contact Pulitzer-Prize-winning author Gene Weingarten, who originally conceived of the stunt, at weingarten@washpost.com.

13. Medina, ibid., p. 74.

14. Marzano, Robert, Pickering, Debra, and Pollock, Jane, *Classroom Instruction That Works* (Alexandria, VA: Association for Supervision and Curriculum Development, 2001), p. 7.

15. I read the $32,000 statistic somewhere but I can no longer find the link. So, for now, this is an unsubstantiated claim but feel free to quote me if it supports your position on the issue.

16. Photo Expansion was developed by the once-flourishing Polaroid Education Project.

17. Eric Dahm is CEO of 100% Educational Videos in Folsom, California, www.schoolvideos.com.

18. www.educatebetter.org/art_wordle.html.

19. I used the Varitronics PosterMaker to print the Wordle in poster size for Emma with white letters on a purple background. Then she colored in the words with pastel marking pens for a beautiful, personalized poster.

20. Amen, Daniel G., *Change Your Brain, Change Your Life: The Breakthrough Program for Conquering Anxiety, Depression, Obsessiveness, Anger, and Impulsiveness* (New York: Three Rivers Press, 1998).

21. http://thinkexist.com/quotation/laughter_is_the_closest_distance_between_two/8403.html.

Chapter 6

1. Activity taken from the author's book, *Visual Literacy: Learn to See, See to Learn* (Alexandria, VA: Association for Supervision and Curriculum Development, 2002), pp. 86–87. Original idea (cited) of a scrambled paragraph from Michael Jursic, a teacher at Ryerson

Community Public School in Toronto, may be found at http://home
.cogeco.ca/~rayser3/joke.txt.

2. Ibid., p. 87.

3. *Neoteny* is defined in Brown, Stuart. (2008). *Why Play Is Vital–No
Matter Your Age* at 14 minutes, 40 seconds. [Available online at:
http://blog.ted.com/2009/03/12/stuart_brown_play].

4. Robertshaw, Dr. Stuart, *Dear Dr. Humor: A Collection of Humor Stories for All Occasions* (La Crosse, WI: National Association for the
Humor Impaired, 1995), p. 3.

5. www.drhumor.com/bio_profile/index.shtml.

6. British actor and comedian John Cleese is the master of this
aspect of humor, as exemplified by the famous sketch in which
he plays a bowler-hatted civil servant in a fictitious British government ministry responsible for developing Silly Walks. The
stuffy outfit and demeanor juxtaposed with the long, gangly,
silly legs make for a hilarious performance. www.youtube.com/
watch?v=lqhlQfXUk7w.

7. Sultanoff, Steven, "Exploring the Land of Mirth and Funny: A
Voyage Through the Interrelationships of Wit, Mirth, and Laughter," *Laugh It Up*, July/August 1994 [Online article available: www
.humormatters.com/articles/explorin.htm].

8. Ibid.

9. From his presentation at the Association for Supervision and Curriculum Development (ASCD) Conference, March 15, 2010, in San
Antonio, Texas.

10. Ibid.

11. If you don't remember it, you know the drill: Just type "herding
cats" into Google or YouTube.

12. Hyena, Hank, "Laugh Loud, Laugh Hard, Live Long," March 31,
2010 [Online article available: www.hplusmagazine.com/articles/
forever-young/laugh-loud-laugh-hard-live-long].

13. Eighteenth-century French Enlightenment author and philoso-
pher Voltaire wrote, "The art of medicine consists of amusing the

patient while nature cures the disease." www.goodreads.com/author/quotes/11619.Voltaire?page=2.

14. Dr. William F. Fry, a leading researcher into the psychology of laughter at Stanford University, says the body gets a healthy "mini-workout" from a good guffaw. He found that it took ten minutes of rowing on his home exercise machine to reach the heart rate produced by one minute of hearty laughter. Fry, William F., "The Physiologic Effects of Humor, Mirth, and Laughter," *Journal of the American Medical Association*, 167(13), 1857–1858.

15. Norman Cousins, author of *Anatomy of an Illness as Perceived by the Patient* (New York: W.W. Norton, 1979), claims he was healed of a diagnosed incurable disease by the power of laughter, which he likened to the exercise of internal jogging. "Hearty laughter is a good way to jog internally without having to go outdoors." www.brainyquote.com/quotes/authors/n/noman_cousins.html.

16. Patch Adams, the real person behind the eponymous 1998 hit movie starring Robin Williams, is both a medical doctor and a clown. He is also a social activist who has devoted forty years of his life to changing America's health care system, a system that he describes as expensive and elitist. He believes that laughter, joy, and creativity are an integral part of the healing process and therefore true health care must incorporate such life. For more information about his work, visit the website: www.patchadams.org/.

17. Hyena, Hank, ibid.

18. Ibid.

19. Photo by Heidi Hoopes. www.flickr.com/photos/meer/23396958/.

20. Founded and maintained by Rushton Hurley, Next Vista for Learning (www.nextvista.org) is dedicated to "changing the world, one video at a time." Subscribe to the free newsletter if you want a smile on your face and some great free resources in your inbox.

21. I first encountered this quote from Dante's *Inferno* over the door of the student whose room was next to mine in the Stanford University dormitory. (She was majoring in Italian and had a distinctly dark sense of humor.) www.brainyquote.com/quotes/authors/d/dante_alighieri.html.

22. Word-for-word Cajun translation of the English expression. Parisians have other ways of expressing this notion.

23. www.quotespapa.com/authors/quincy-jones-quotes.html. (Scroll down to Score 56.)

Chapter 7

1. Learn more about J. Howard Miller's famous poster and the women who worked in munitions manufacturing plants during World War II: www.u-s-history.com/pages/h1656.html.

2. www.speakingaboutpresenting.com.

3. 3M Corporation research cited in "Polishing Your Presentation," *3M Meeting Network Articles & Advice,* 2001 [Online article was posted at: www.em.com/meetingnetwork/readingroom/meeting-guide_pres.html].

4. Burmark, Lynell, *Visual Literacy,* p. 8.

5. Atkinson, Cliff, *Beyond Bullet Points* (Redmond, WA: Microsoft Press, 2005), pp. 51, 53.

6. Velcro photomicrograph from Tracy Anderson, University of Minnesota. Used with permission.

7. Johnson, Tom, www.idratherbewriting.com cited by Duarte, *slide:ology,* p. 227.

8. Atkinson, p. 53.

9. Duarte, Nancy, *slide:ology,* pp. 222–223.

10. Reynolds, Garr, *Presentation Zen Design,* p. 100.

11. Ibid., p. 101.

12. www.istockphoto.com.

13. Reynolds, Garr, ibid., p. 141.

14. Ibid., p. 173.

15. Ibid.

16. Margaret Lew's *Bouquets to Art* photographs from the 2007 and 2008 shows are posted at www.pbase.com/mclew/flower_show.

17. The eye goes to color before black and white, to images before data.

18. The image of "Velcro Dog" used with permission from Johny Day. Visit his photostream for more great and tender-hearted photos: www.flickr.com/photos/johnydaystudio/.

19. A longer version of the "Three Little Pigs" story (with blanks to fill in with *there, their,* or *they're*) is posted on the Outta Ray's Head website under Lesson Plans for Writing: http://home.cogeco.ca/˜rayser3/writing.htm#their.

20. This photograph, titled "Gettysburg Hero," is part of the Mathew Brady collection you can access through the American Memory Project: http://memory.loc.gov/ammem/cwphtml/cwphome.html.

21. 3M Corporation research cited in "The Power of Color in Presentations," *3M Meeting Network Articles & Advice*, 2001 [Online article was posted at: www.3m.com/meetingnetwork/readingroom/meetingguide_pwer_color.html].

22. "Investigating the Effects of Color, Fonts, and Bold Text in Documents," Working Paper #WP0196.029 by investigative researchers Ellen D. Hoadley, Laurette Simons, and Faith Gilroy at the David D. Lattanze Center for Executive Studies in Information Systems, Loyola College, Baltimore, Maryland, 1995 [Online article was posted at: www.accentcolor.com/products/wp0196.029.html].

23. Medina, John, *Brain Rules*, p. 234.

24. Ibid., p. 233.

25. Dick and Jane were the main characters in popular basal readers published by Scott Foresman and used to teach children to read from the 1930s through to the 1970s in the United States. www.rarebookschool.org/2005/exhibitions/dickandjane.shtml.

26. Medina, ibid.

27. Nin, Anaïs, "We don't see things as they are. We see them as we are." www.goodreads.com/author/quotes/7190.Ana_s_Nin.

28. Burmark, Lynell, *Visual Literacy: Learn to See, See to Learn*, p. 9 [Available from: www.educatebetter.org/publications.html].

29. Rakes, Glenda C., "Teaching Visual Literacy in a Multimedia Age," *TechTrends*, 43, September 1999, pp. 14–15.

30. Mayer, Richard E., *Multimedia Learning*.

31. Photographs courtesy of Rashmi Sinha. Used with permission.

Chapter 8

1. Visit YouTube for classic clips or purchase DVDs with archival restoration to experience jewels of this genre. www.silentera .com/store/index.html.

2. /www.musica.uci.edu/mrn/V8I1W01.html#feel.

3. Ibid.

4. Each clip is approximately three minutes in length. All clips are original compositions by Lou Marzeles and provided on this book's DVD royalty-free for educational use only.

5. www.bonniestjohn.com/.

6. www.youtube.com/watch?v=v-17NWRddUk.

7. Also provided on this book's DVD royalty-free for educational use only.

8. Ohler, Jason, *Digital Storytelling in the Classroom* (Thousand Oaks, CA: Corwin Press, 2008), p. 186.

9. Ibid., p. 187.

10. http://disneyland.disney.go.com/disneys-california-adventure/ soarin/

11. "The last of human freedoms to choose one's attitude in any given set of circumstances, to choose one's own way."—Viktor E. Frankl. www.inspiredprojectteams.com/?p=1026. "The most courageous decision one makes each day is to be in a good mood."—Voltaire. www.goodreads.com/quotes/show/313868.

12. Krumhansl, Carol, "An Exploratory Study of Musical Emotions and Psychophysiology," *Canadian Journal of Experiential Psychology,* 51, 336–352. Examples of selections were "Spring" from "The Four Seasons" by Vivaldi (happy), "Adagio for Strings" by Samuel Barber (sad), and "Night on Bald Mountain" by Mussorgsky (fear).

13. McCraty, Rollin, *Science of the Heart* (Boulder Creek, CO: Institute of HeartMath, 2001), pp. 30–32.

14. "The Green Days" segment of *Dr. Seuss' My Many Colored Days* video performed by the Minnesota Orchestra. www.amazon .com/Seusss-Many-Colored-Notes-Alive/dp/1893274004.

15. In the music folder on the DVD that accompanies this book original compositions by Lou Marzeles are provided royalty-free for educational use only .

16. Bortz, Walter M. *Dare to Be 100* (New York: Simon and Schuster, 1996), p. 164.

17. Ibid.

18. www.foxnews.com/us/2010/09/08/instrument-shortage-leaves-california-school-band-singing-blues/.

19. Weinberger, Norman M., "Threads of Music in the Tapestry of Memory" 1997 [Online article available: www.musica.uci.edu/mrn/ V4I1S97.html#threads].

20. Balch, William, "Music-Dependent Memory: The Roles of Tempo Change and Mood Mediation," *Journal for Experiential Psychology, Learning, Memory & Cognition,* 22, 1354–1363.

21. Research by T. Taniguchi of Kyoto University as cited by Norman W. Weinberger, in "The Coloring of Life: Music and Mood" 1996 [Online article available: www.musica.uci.edu/mrn/V3I1S96. html#coloring.

22. www.waterfordearlylearning.org/overview.html].

23. Although this wonderful video is out of print, teachers can offer musically inclined students the option of performing the way Leah did. And today they will probably post their performances on YouTube!

24. www.greatquotesmovie.com.

Chapter 9

1. Medina, John, *Brain Rules*, p. 81.

2. Truman, Karol K., *Feelings Buried Alive Never Die* (Las Vegas, NV: Olympus Distributing, 1991), pp. 177–202.

3. Reynolds, Garr, *Presentation Zen*, pp. 20–21. Also, visit www .sethgodin.com.

4. Godin, Seth, "Really Bad Powerpoint," Seth's Blog. http://sethgodin .typepad.com/seths_blog/2007/01/really_bad_powe.html.

5. Ibid.

6. Heath, Chip, and Heath, Dan, *Made to Stick*, pp. 166–167.

7. Ibid.

8. http://eideneurolearningblog.blogspot.com/2010/06/emotions-and-humor-in-learning-and.html.

9. www.historyplace.com/unitedstates/childlabor.

10. Visit Dave Carroll's website for details on the United Breaks Guitars story [www.davecarrollmusic.com/ubg/story/], to listen to the song [www.davecarrollmusic.com/ubg/song1/], and to enjoy lyrics and samples from more of his music such as "Now" from the "Perfect Blue" album: www.davecarrollmusic.com/music/perfectblue/now/.

11. Medina, John, *Brain Rules*, p. 185.

12. Ibid.

13. Glazier, Stephen, *Word Menu* (New York: Random House, 1998).

14. Ibid., p. 670.

15. www.wordle.net.

16. http://commfaculty.fullerton.edu/lester/writings/gerald.html.

17. www.heartmath.org/research/research-home/research-center-home.html.

18. Childre, Doc, and Martin, Howard, *The HeartMath Solution* (San Francisco: HarperCollins, 1999), p. 34.

19. Greer, Michael, "10 Specific Actions That Can Help You Become Happier," *Inspired Project Teams*. www.inspiredprojectteams .com/?p=1122.

20. As measured by PET scans of the brain and chemical tests of the saliva; Childre, Doc, and Martin, Howard, *The HeartMath Solution*.

Chapter 10

1. www.scientificamerican.com/blog/post.cfm?id=of-two-minds-listener-brain-pattern-2010-07-27.

2. www.newscientist.com/article/dn19220-we-humans-can-mind-meld-too.html.

3. Stephens, Greg J., Silbert, Lauren J., and Hasson, Uri, "Speaker-Listener Neural Coupling Underlies Successful Communication," *Proceedings of the National Academy of Sciences,* June 18, 2010 [Online article available: www.pnas.org/content/107/32/14425.full].

4. Visit Sara's website at www.sgaconsulting.org/.

5. Ohler, Jason, *Digital Storytelling in the Classroom* (Thousand Oaks, CA: Corwin Press, 2008), p. 182.

6. Ibid, p. 9.

7. Turner, Mark, *The Literary Mind: The Origins of Thought and Language* (New York: Oxford University Press, 1966), pp. 4–5.

8. Heath, Chip, and Heath, Dan, *Made to Stick*, p. 109.

9. Ibid., p. 73.

10. Shared in the sermon "Hope Springs Eternal" given on March 3, 2002, by the Reverend Doctor J. Edwin Bacon, Jr., at All Saints Church in Pasadena, California. Reprinted with permission.

11. www.philosophersguild.com.

12. www.amazon.com/Button-Down-Mind-Bob-Newhart/dp/ B000002MSU.

13. *Sacagawea* DVD available www.schoolvideos.com.

14. Bolles, Richard Nelson, *What Color Is Your Parachute? A Practical Manual for Job-Hunters and Career-Changers.*

15. Bolles, Richard Nelson, *The What Color Is Your Parachute Workshop,* Bend, Oregon, July 28–August 13, 2000.

16. Truss, Lynne, *Eats, Shoots & Leaves: The Zero Tolerance Approach to Punctuation* (New York: Gotham Books, 2004).

17. www.radicalplatypus.com/.

18. After twenty-six years with the Walt Disney Company (creating theme-park experiences), Bob Allen founded the innovation studio IDEAS in Orlando, Florida. Bob is a playful storyteller and a conceptual futurist. http://ideasorlando.com/ideas/profiles/bob-allen/.

19. www.edutopia.org/blog/teams-jim-brazell-the-universe.

20. animoto.com/play/sQAQG1ofStlUaG3emoJO9Q.

21. Porter, Bernajean, Digitalstorytellers Special Interest Group Meeting, International Society for Technology in Education (ISTE) annual conference, Denver, CO, June 29, 2010.

Chapter 11

1. Mayer, Richard E., *Multimedia Learning.*

2. Ibid., p. 63.

3. Paivio, Allan, *Mental Representations: A Dual-Coding Approach* (Oxford, UK: Oxford University Press, 1986).

4. Baddeley, Alan, *Human Memory* (Boston: Allyn & Bacon, 1999).

5. Chandler, Paul, and Sweller, John, "Cognitive Load Theory and the Format of Instruction," *Cognition and Instruction*, 1991, 8, 293–332.

6. Mayer, ibid., pp. 52–53.

7. "Students perform better on transfer tests when they learn from words and pictures than when they learn from words alone." Ibid., p. 274

8. Regarding the modality principle: "In seventeen out of seventeen tests, people performed better on problem-solving transfer tests when an animation or set of graphics was accompanied by narration rather than on-screen text." Ibid., p. 200

9. As for redundancy, when one might assume that hearing *and* seeing the text is better, all five studies that Mayer conducted showed that "people learn more deeply from graphics and narration than from graphics, narration, and printed text [because] the graphics and printed text are overloading the visual channel. Ibid., p. 127.

10. Medina, John, *Brain Rules*, p. 74.

11. Mayer, ibid., p. 55.

12. www.amazon.com/Chocolovers-Aquolina-Women-Toilette-Spray/dp/B000JLEZ06.

13. According to new research published in the medical journal *Lancet*, dark chocolate is now considered a health food. Similar to tea, it has antioxidants that could prevent cancer. Similar to red wine, it reduces the buildup of plaque in the arteries, a major cause of heart attacks.

    Most of the bad press on chocolate is either overstated or entirely false. For example, chocolate has *not* been proved to cause cavities or tooth decay. The cocoa butter in the chocolate actually coats the teeth and prevents plaque from forming. Plus parts of a cocoa bean work to thwart mouth bacteria.

    And, really, how can savoring one little square a day make you obese? Just don't eat the whole bar or consume your chocolate as frosting on donuts. No amount of rationalization makes that a healthy snack.

    (Liberally adapted from www.manbir-online.com/nutrition/chocolate.htm.)

14. Chocolate quiz:

    • Which medical journal recently published an article on the benefits of dark chocolate?

    • Similar to what beverage does it help prevent cancer?

    • Similar to what beverage does it help prevent arterial plaque and heart attacks?

- True or false: Does chocolate promote tooth decay?
- Name one healthy and one unhealthy way to consume chocolate.

15. Medina, ibid., p. 217.

16. Ibid., pp. 211–212.

17. Anderson, Kare, "Coming Back to Our Senses to Create More Memorable Meetings" [Online article available: www.presentation-pointers.com/printarticle.asp?articleid=2].

18. From *À La Recherche du Temps Perdu* (*Remembrance of Things Past*), Proust's autobiographical novel told mostly in a stream-of-consciousness style. The novel is composed of seven volumes, the first of which, *Du Côté de Chez Swann* (*Swann's Way*), was published by Grasset Paris in 1913. The first part of that volume, *Combray I*, ends with the famous "madeleine cookie" episode, introducing the theme of involuntary memory.

19. Lindstrom, Martin, "Designing Ambiance," *Create Magazine*, Fall 2005 [Online article available: http://adholes.com/postings/dc2576f8841b87523cbc92ba00389ab5].

20. Ibid.

21. Lehrner, J., Eckersberger, C., Walla, P., Potsch, G., and Deecke, L., "Ambient Odor of Orange in a Dental Office Reduces Anxiety and Improves Mood in Female Patients," *Physiological Behavior*, August 10, 2005, 71, 83–86.

22. Lindstrom, ibid.

23. Eeva Reeder now works for the school design firm of Fielding and Nair consulting on optimal environments for learning math.

24. Baines, Lawrence, *Multisensory Learning* (Alexandria, VA: Association for Supervision and Curriculum Development, 2008).

25. Medina, ibid., p. 208.

26. www2.ed.gov/pubs/EPTW/eptw4/eptw4e.html.

27. Stewart, Melissa, "From Tangerines to Algorithms," *Instructor*, April 2003 [Online article available: www2.scholastic.com/browse/article.jsp?id=3915].

28. Lindstrom, ibid.

29. Ibid.

30. Lemons have long been praised for boosting memory. Their bright, clean scent is said to aid in information storage and recall. http://mindbodyfitness.suite101.com/article.cfm/aromatherapy-to-enhance-your-memory.

    Note: The lemon photo is copyrighted by Rob Tunstall and used here with permission. The "If life throws you a lemon . . ." image can be found on his photostream at www.flickr.com/photos/baldmonk/2302950648/.

31. Lindstrom, ibid.

Chapter 12

1. Duarte, Nancy, *slide:ology*, pp. 222–223.

2. Koosh balls are available in a variety of sizes, shapes, and prices from www.orientaltrading.com. My favorite is the "worm ball," which is softer and more fun to play with than the smaller, less expensive "porcupine ball."

3. Marzano, Robert, Pickering, Debra, and Pollock, Jane, *Classroom Instruction That Works*, p. 7.

4. Medina, John, *Brain Rules*, p. 221.

5. www.heartmath.org/research/science-of-the-heart/head-heart-interactions.html.

6. The *Sacagawea* DVD is available from www.schoolvideos.com.

7. www.schooltube.com/video/0004acc0553a4d7ab592/Matrix-Learning-Bad-Date-by-NMSU.

8. www.SimpleTruths.com.

9. ADOSS was first explained to me by Rushton Hurley, who claims he was diagnosed with an adult-onset version of the condition.

Index

A

"Abe Lincoln versus Madison Avenue" (Newhart), 185

Adams, Patch, 102, 238

Africa, 160

Ainsworth, Larry, 61

"Ain't No Sunshine When She's Gone" (song), 149

Alameda County Office of Education (Hayward, California), 204

Alighieri, Dante, 105, 238

"All My Exes Live in Texas" (country song), 107

Allen, Bob, 191, 193, 245

"Ambience for Learning" (presentation; Burmark), 144

Amen, Daniel, 87

"America's New Deadly Obsession" (Oprah), 36

Anatomy of an Illness as Perceived by the Patient (Cousins), 238

Anderson, Kare, 202

Andy Griffith Show (television series), 129

Antibes Seen from the Salis Gardens (painting; Monet), 8

Apollo Ideas (slideshow; Brenman), 13–14

Apple Computer, 43, 47, 49

Arial typeface, 15, 19, 232

Armstrong, Sara, 177

Armstrong, Thomas, 234

ASCD. See Association for Supervision and Curriculum Development (ASCD)

"Ashokan Farewell" (traditional song), 151

Association for Supervision and Curriculum Development (ASCD), 11, 148; Conference (Chicago), 26; Conference (San Antonio, Texas), 54

Atkinson, Cliff, 115

Attention Deficit Disorder (ADD), 62

Avatar (film), 145–146

B

Bach, J. S., 141

"Bad Date" (animation), 70, 225, 234

Baines, Lawrence, 207

Ballou, Sarah, 151

Ballou, Sullivan, 151

Bambi (film), 144

Barclay's PLC, 203

Bauer, Dave, 14–18

Baumgartner, Cathy, 224

Beatles (rock group), 153

Bee Gees (rock group), 142

"Believe" (song), 44

Bell, Joshua (violinist), 78

Berk, Lee, 102

Beyond Bullet Points (Atkinson), 115

Big Horn Mountains, 55

Blaha, Dustin, 85

Bodily-kinesthetic senses, 204–206

Bolles, Richard N., 66, 67, 167, 186, 188–189, 235

Borge, Victor, 91

Botanical Gardens (Atlanta, Georgia), 103, 197

"Bouquets to Art" (De Young Museum), 125

Boyle, Susan (singer), 65

Brady, Matthew, 129–130

Brain Rules (Medina), 5, 78

BRANDSense (Lindstrom), 203, 204

Brazell, Jim, 53, 190, 191, 193

Brenman, Jeff, 13, 14

Brennan, Jim, 25

Britain's Got Talent, 65

British Petroleum PLC, 180

Broderick, Matthew, 43

Brooks, Tanisha, 74

Brut, 202

Buck, Pearl S., 39–40

Buffalo, Wyoming, 55

Bullets, 1

Bunzel, Jack, 136

Burg, Jerome, 172

Burmark, Lynell, 34, 61, 89, 115, 122, 144, 215, 226

Burmark, Wes, 73, 106

Burns, Ken, 151

Business Week, 47

Button-Down Mind of Bob Newhart (Newhart), 185

C

Caesars Palace (Las Vegas, Nevada), 44

California Adventure (Disney), 144

Cameron, James, 145–146

Campbell, Bruce, 152

"Can't Take My Eyes Off of You" (YouTube), 110

Cardenas, Mäida, 77, 79

Carroll, Dave, 164–165

Celtic Woman (musical ensemble), 143

Change Your Brain, Change Your Life (Amen), 87

Chaplin, Charlie, 141

Charles, Ray, 152

Charles II (Great Britain), 102

Cheers (television series), 82, 141

Cher (popular singer), 44, 46, 82

Cher: Live in Concert from Las Vegas, 44

CHIMES², 66

Chocolate, 246–247

Chocolovers (Aqulina Perfume), 201, 202

Cinderella fairy tale, 235

Cirque du Soleil, 114, 124

Civil War (documentary series), 151

Classroom Instruction That Works (Marzano), 80

Cleese, John, 102, 103, 237

Clinton, Bill, 45–46

Cloud Appreciation Society, 74–75

Coggan, Darian, 25

"Cognitive Style of PowerPoint: Pitching Out Corrupts Within" (Tufte), 229

Color, 7–11; and images, 126–132

"Color Matters" (website; Morton), 10

Comedy Club, 101

Comparing and contrasting, 80–81

Complementary, 28, 32, 232

Computer-Using Educators (CUE), 5

"Conceptual Age" (Pink), 231

Connections, making, 69–92; and 10:2 practice, 78–80; and breaking language barrier, 90–91; and building on prior knowledge, 74–78; and comparing and contrasting, 80–81; and making abstract concrete, 70–74; and name recognition, 82–87; and physical connection, 87–90; using humor for, 91–92

Content, 100–107

Context, creating, 222–223

Cornell University, 146

Cosby, Bill, 152

Cosby Show, The (television show), 152

Cousins, Norman, 102, 238

Creative Commons license, 104

Crunchem Hall Elementary School, 93, 95

CUE. *See* Computer-Using Educators (CUE)

Culver Academies (Culver, Indiana), 87

D

Dahm, Eric, 84

Dairy Queen, 73

Danson, Ted, 82

Davidson, Hall, 206

De Anza College (Cupertino, California), 90

de Mestral, George, 64

De Young Museum (San Francisco, California), 125

Dear Dr. Humor (Robertshaw), 96

Deliverance (film), 141–142

Denver, John, 149

Dick and Jane (fictional characters), 132, 240

Digital flash cards, 76

Dion, Céline, 45, 46

Discovery Education, 206

Disney World (Orlando, Florida), 144

Disneyland (Anaheim, California), 144

Dolby surround sound, 141

Dollar Store, 211

"Don't Believe My Heart Can Stand Another You" (country song), 107

Dr. Seuss, 97

Dual-coding, 133

Duarte, Nancy, 4, 5, 11, 14, 21, 33, 116–117, 217, 230

E

"Earthlights" (NASA), 10

Edutainment presentations, 25, 26

Eide, Brock, 161

Eide, Fernette, 161

Einstein, Alfred, 192

El Greco, 28

Emotion: engaging, 224–225; and feeling words, 158–174; and music, 144–148; tapping, 157–174

Emotional photo wall, 225

"Enlighten Up!" (song), 144

Entertainment presentations, 25, 26

Envisioning Information (Tufte), 10

Epson Corporation, 80

Escalante, Jaime, 26

Ethical Culture School (New York City), 162

Excel, 73

F

Facebook, 35

Feelings Buried Alive Never Die (Truman), 157

Ferris Bueller's Day Off (film), 43, 44

Fiori, Louise, 209

Fish Called Wanda (film), 102

Fisherman's House at Varengeville (painting; Monet), 8

5 Minute University (YouTube), 61

Flickr (online photo management), 104–105

Flint Center (De Anza College), 90

Floss Fairy, 61

"Flowers Exercise," 66–67

Foresman, Scott, 240

4 Generations (video), 39

Frankl, Viktor E., 241

Fremont Unified School District (California), 77

French Impressionist painters, 8

Freymiller, Susan, 87

Friends (television series), 141

Fry, William, F., 102, 238

Functional magnetic resonance imaging (fMRI), 176–177

G

G., Kenney (musician), 90

Gallo, Carmine, 47–48

Gandhi, M., 1

Ganzel, Rebecca, 229

Gardner, Howard, 54–55, 209, 234

Gauguin, Paul, 173

Georgia typeface, 19, 232

"Glance media," 14

Godin, Seth, 159

Golden Gate Bridge (San Francisco, California), 144

Goldsmith, Jerry, 144

Good Earth (Buck), 39–40

Google, 62, 81, 105, 122, 170, 226

Gore, Al, 5, 230

Graham, Billy, 44, 46

Grateful Dead (rock group), 150

Great Depression, 96

Great Philosophers finger puppets, 184

Great Quotes Movie (Simple Truths), 153

Grimmer Elementary School (Fremont, California), 77, 79

Grow, Gerald, 169

Gulf of Mexico oil spill (2010), 180

"Gypsies, Tramps & Thieves" (song), 44

H

Hallowell, Edward, 62

Handouts: creating, 32–33; length of, 33; online, 35–37. *See also* Slides and handouts, creating

Hasson, Uri, 177

Hearing, 196–200

HeartMath, 172, 224

HeartMath Solution (Childre and Martin), 172

Heath, Chip, 4, 70, 182, 230

Heath, Dan, 4, 70, 182, 230

Helvetica typeface, 15, 21

"Here Comes the Sun" (rock song), 143

Hine, Lewis W., 161–163

Historical events, sequencing, 75

Historical perspective, 98

Honeycutt, Debbie, 149

Hot Pockets, 62

Humor: for connecting, 91–92; and content, 100–107; defining, 98–100; harnessing, 93–107; and historical perspective, 98; infusing, 223; and neoteny, 95–97; with recall, 75; and surprise, 97–98

Hurley, Rushton, 238

Hyatt Regency, 55

Hyena, Hank, 102

HyperStudio, 25, 198, 230

I

"I Can't Stop Loving You" (song), 152

"I Got Through Everything but the Door" (country song), 107

"I Got You Babe" (song), 44

"I Have a Dream" speech (King), 223

IDEAS innovation studio, 245

Illustration, 115–116

Image-Making within the Writing Process program, 208

Images: and color, 126–132; combining words with, 132–140; and focusing on essentials, 116–119; for illustration, 115–116; and setting stage, 113–115; sizing and placing, 119–126; starting with, 109–140

Immediacy, 34–35

Inconvenient Truth, An (documentary; Gore), 5, 230

India, 137

Individualized Education Plan (IEP), 87

Inferences, 112

Inferno (Dante), 105, 238

Institute of Heart Math (Colorado), 147

Instructor magazine, 209

Internal Revenue Service (IRS), 21

International Society for Technology in Education (ISTE), 34; Conference (Denver), 84

iPod, 78, 150

iStockphoto CopySpace, 122

J

Jaws (film), 144

Jensen, Stacie, 223

Jobs, Steve, 43, 47–49, 52, 53; ten tips from, 48

Johnson, George, 87

Johnson, Tom, 116

Jolie, Angelina, 82

Jonas, Peter, 100

Jones, Quincy, 107

Journey Back (Reiss), 152

Jursic, Michael, 93

K

"K-12 Education in Five Minutes or Less" (Burmark), 61

Kahlo, Frida, 77

Kanyangereka, Tanzania, 102

Kashasha, Tanzania, 102

Kaye, Danny, 167

Keaton, Buster, 141

Keller, Helen, 92

Kerala, India, 28, 137, 139

Kerala State Tourism Bureau, 138

Kerning, 15, 20, 232

King, Martin Luther, Jr., 186, 223

Kinko's, 33

Koosh ball, 181, 182, 220, 248

Krazy Glue, 224

Krumhansl, Carol, 146

L

Lake Tahoe (California), 144

Lancet, 246

Language barrier, 90–91

"Lara's Song" (song), 141

Laughter, 98, 100, 238

Lawrence of Arabia (film), 141

LCD projectors, 222, 227

Leave It to Beaver (television series), 129

Ledger, Heath, 110

Lemons, 248

Les Misérables (Hugo), 116

Lewis and Clark expedition, 96, 185, 225

Lindstrom, Martin, 203, 204, 210

Lion King (Broadway show), 114

Little Rock, Arkansas, 99

Liverpool, England, 153

Liverpool Institute for Performing Arts (LIPA), 154–155

Loma Linda University (California), 102

Los Angeles, California, 164

Louisiana, 180

M

Mackie, Bob, 44

Macworld, 53

Madame Charpentier with Her Children (Renoir), 28

Made to Stick: Why Some Ideas Survive and Others Die (Heath and Heath), 182, 230

"Making Education Stick" workshop (Burmark), 122

Mali, Africa, 160

Marzano, Robert, 53–54, 61, 80, 222

Marzeles, Lou, 144

MASH (television series), 141

Mass Psychogenic Illness (MPI), 103

Mayer, Richard E., 28, 30, 33, 134, 199, 200, 245, 246

McCartney, Paul, 154

McNeils, Michael, 162

McREL. *See* Mid-continent Research for Education and Learning (McREL)

Meddybumps website,77

Medina, John, 5, 12, 26, 33, 35, 78, 79, 165, 202, 222

Mid-continent Research for Education and Learning (McREL), 53–54

Middle Ages, 7

Middlestadt, Doug, 99

Mirth, 98, 99

Mitchell, Olivia, 114

Moby Dick (Melville), 116

Modality principle, 246

Mona Lisa, 77

Monet, Claude, 8, 9, 141

Monterey Bay (California), 144

Mood, 151

"Moody Melody" (song), 149

Morton, J. L., 10

Moscone Center (San Francisco, California), 53

Mountlake Terrace School District (Washington), 204

Multimedia Learning (Mayer), 30, 199, 246

Multiple intelligences, 54–55, 234

Multiple Intelligences in the Classroom (Campbell), 152

Multiple senses, 209–212

Multisensory Learning (Baines), 207

Music, playing, 141–156, 221

"My Heart Will Go On" (song), 45, 141

My Name is Cholera (Coggan), 25

N

Name recognition, 82–87

National Child Labor Committee (NCLC), 162–163

National Oceanic and Atmospheric Administration (NOAA), 29

National School Boards Association Teaching and Learning Conference (NSBA T+L), 62

Neotenous pranks, 96

Neoteny, 95–97, 237

New York Times, 46, 182

Next Vista for Learning, 105, 238

Nielson, Jakob, 25

Nightingale, Florence, 150

Nin, Anaïs, 133

No Me Queda Mas (song; Selena), 164

NOAA. *See* National Oceanic and Atmospheric Administration (NOAA)

Nordstrom, 182

Nshamba, Tanzania, 102

O

Ohler, Jason, 179

Oliver Wendell Holmes Foundation Academy (Flint, Michigan), 74

Oprah, 36, 45

Oriental Trading Company, 89

Orr, Leah, 152

Osment, Haley Joel, 46

P

Paivio, Allan, 133, 134

Passion, 221

Pay It Forward (film), 46

Peale, Norman Vincent, 122, 123

Pearson Executive Forum (San Diego, California), 91

Photo Expansion project, 82, 83

PhotoShop, 6, 12, 121

Picasso, Pablo, 20

Pilates, 149

Pink, Daniel, 4, 230–231

Pitler, Howard, 53–54

Plato, 150

Play-Doh, 191–192

PlayShops (Bolles and Allen), 191

Point of view, 110, 111

Porter, Bernajean, 193

Portmanteau, 64–65, 234

Positron emission tomography (PET scans), 134

Post-it notes, 157

"Power of Visuals in Teaching and Learning" (presentation; Burmark), 226

Power Standards (Ainsworth), 61

PowerPoint, 3–5, 12, 18

"PowerPointless" (Ganzel), 229

Presentation Secrets of Steve Jobs: How To Be Insanely Great in Front of Any Audience (Gallo), 47

Presentation Zen (Reynolds), 5, 229

Presentation Zen Design (Reynolds), 229

Presentation Zero (Reynolds), 123

Presentations, tweaking, 3–24; and color, 7–11; quantity then quality in, 15–23; and templates, 5–6; and type, 11–14

Presentations Magazine, 229

Presenters, celebrating, 43–57

Presley, Elvis, 153

Prince (rock star), 82

Princeton University, 176

Prioritizing Grid (Bolles), 67

Progressive Story activity, 180

Proust, Marcel, 203, 210, 247

Proust effect, 203

PSE (pictorial superiority effect), 131

Public domain, 104

Puns, 99

R

Rabelais, 102

Radical Platypus, 190

Rakes, Glenda, 134

Random House Webster's Word Menu, 167, 168

Rapid City, South Dakota, school district, 85

Rapid Fire activity, 136–140

Rashad, Phylicia, 152

Red Bull International Air Race, 124

Redundant, 28, 232, 246

Reeder, Eeva, 204

References, 33

Regan, Ronald, 100

Reiss, Johanna, 152

Remembrance of Things Past (Proust), 247

Renoir, Pierre-Auguste, 28

Replication, 32

Resolution, 213–228; and changing up, 220–221; and creating context, 222–223; and engaging emotions, 224–225; and following passion, 221; and infusing humor, 223; and making handout, 220; and playing music, 221; and putting it all together, 215–228; and starting with concrete, 219–220; and telling stories, 226–228; and tweaking text, 216–219; and well-formatted text, 218

Reynolds, Garr, 4, 5, 33, 122–124, 229

Robbins, Tim, 45–46

Robertshaw, Stuart, 96

Rocky (film), 144

Rose, David S., 70, 74

Ryerson Community Public School (Toronto, Canada), 93

S

Sacagawea, 96, 185, 186, 225

Sacramento, California, 150–151

Sarducci, Father Guido (comedian), 61, 62

Saturday Night Live (television show), 61, 142

Save the Children Foundation, 160

SchoolTube, 70, 105, 225

Scott Lane Elementary School (Santa Clara, California), 82, 151

Senses: and bodily-kinesthetic senses, 204–206; engaging, 195–212; and multiple senses, 209–212; and smell, 201–204; and taste, 206; and touch, 207–209; and vision and hearing, 196–200

Sensogram (Lindstrom), 210

Shakespeare, William, 110

Silicon Valley, California, 227

Simons, Tad, 4

Simple Truths, 153, 225

"Six Sides of Shanta" (presentation), 198–200, 210, 211

Skelton, Red, 167

Skyline Junior High School, 152

slide:ology: The Art and Science of Great Presentations (Duarte), 5, 116–117, 217, 230

Slides and handouts, creating, 25–41; and handouts, 32–33; and immediacy, 34–35; job of, 28–32; and length of handouts, 33; and online handout, 35–37; and references, 33; on stage, 26–27; on their heads, 27–28; on web, 25; words in, 37–41

Slideshare.net, 115

Slumdog Millionaire (film), 141

Smell, 201–204

"Soaring over California" (California Adventure ride), 144, 145

Spacey, Kevin, 46

Speed and Balance (song), 147

Spokane, Washington, 88

St. John, Bonnie, 26, 143

Stadium High School (Tacoma, Washington), 110, 113

Stage, setting, 113–115

Stanford University, 10, 136

"Stayin' Alive" (rock song), 142

Stein, Ben, 43

Stiles, Julia, 110

Stills, 135

Stop and Hear the Music (YouTube), 78

Stories: and prioritizing skills, 188–193; telling, 175–193, 226–228; and trioing, 188; writing, 186–188

Strager, Gary, 176

Sullivan, Annie, 92

Sultanoff, Stephen, 98

Sunflowers (Van Gogh), 173

Sunlight Effect Under the Poplars (painting; Monet), 8

"Sunshine on My Shoulders" (song), 149

Surprise, 97–98

Symphony Hall (Boston, Massachusetts), 78

Synergistic, 28, 233

T

Tacoma, Washington, 106, 223; Public Schools, 73, 154

Tacoma School of the Arts (TSOTA), 154–155

Takahashi huge-text method, 13

Taming of the Shrew (Shakespeare), 110

Tanzania, 102, 103

Task-switching, 36

Taste, 206

Teach It Forward (TIF) plan, 47

TeacherTube, 105

"Teaching Visual Literacy in a Multimedia Age" (Rakes), 134

"Technology Velcro" (presentation; Burmark), 34

TEDtalks, 44

TEL•A•VISION, 87

Templates, 5–6

Tempo, 151

"Ten Shots to Caffeinate Your Presentations" (Burmark), 215

10 Things I Hate About You (film), 110

10:2 practice, 78–80

Texas Computer Education Association (TCEA), 226

Text: tweaking, 216–219; well-formatted, 218

Thirst (slideshow; Brennan), 25

This Is Your Life (Burmark), 73

"This Little Light of Mine" (song), 3

Thornburg, David, 5

3M Corporation, 7, 157

Tigard, Oregon, 50, 97

Times New Roman font, 19, 232

Titanic (film), 45, 141, 145–146

Tolle, Eckhart, 37, 44

Touch, 207–209

Travolta, John, 142

Trebuchet typeface, 15

Truman, Karol K., 157

Tufte, Edward, 4, 10, 229

Tupelo, Mississippi, 153

Twain, Mark, 99

Typeface, 11–14, 19–23

U

Ultimate Edge (Robbins), 45

United Airlines, 164

"United Breaks Guitars" (Carroll), 164

United States Treasury, 21

University of California, Berkeley, 10

University of California, Irvine, 141

University of California, Santa Barbara, 28

University of Minnesota School of Management, 7

University of Washington, 202

University of Western Ontario, 133

Upstairs Room (Reiss), 152

Urquhart, Sir Thomas, 102

V

Van Gogh, Vincent, 173

Varkala Beach (Kerala, India), 28, 138, 139

Vehicular dialect, 90

Velcro, 55, 64, 65, 115, 182

"Veni, Vidi, Velcro (I Came, I Saw, I Stuck)" (presentation; Burmark), 115

Verdana typeface, 19, 76, 232

View of Toledo in a Storm (painting; El Greco), 28

Virgin Mary, 7

Vision, 196–200

Visual Literacy: Learn to See, See to Learn (Association for Supervision and Curriculum Development), 11

Visualtrack, 135

Voltaire, 102, 237–238, 241

W

Wagner, Carlton, 8, 33

Wagner, Roger, 4, 230

War and Peace (Tolstoy), 116

Warner Brothers, 46

Waterford Early Reading Program, 151

"We Can Do It" World War II propaganda poster, 111, 113, 119

Weinberger, Norman, 141, 142

Wendt, George, 82

What Color Is Your Parachute? A Practical Manual for Job-Hunters and Career-Changers (Bolles), 67, 167, 186, 189

Whole New Mind: Why Right-Brainers Will Rule the Future (Pink), 230–231

Wikimedia, 105

Williams, Robin (comedian), 238

Winfrey, Oprah, 45

Wit, 98

Withers, Bill, 149

Wordle, 84–87

Words Worth 1000 Pictures (Grow), 169

World War II, 111

Wormwood, Matilda, 93

WXGA projectors, 80, 120, 122

X

XGA resolution, 80, 120, 121

Y

Yosemite National Park, 144

"You Fill Up My Senses" (presentation; Burmark), 89

"You Raise Me Up" (song), 143

YouTube, 18, 47, 65, 78, 105, 110, 114, 144, 155, 164

Illustration credits

Note: Photographs taken by the author and from royalty-free websites are not listed. This is just a place to explain the origin of particular images and to acknowledge and cite photographers as requested.

Page	Description	Source/Info/Photograph by
1	Gandhi	www.dinodia.com
6	Template, dog kibble	Drawn by the author as a simulation
12	Medina 40	Photoshop altered book cover.
20	Picasso quote	Adapted from www.slideshare.net/toddchandler/7-quotes-about-mothers
51	Worms	Adrian Brophy
51	Blue eggs	Joan Kovatch
57	Applause	Lance Cadena
59	Velcro	Tracy E. Anderson
64	Burrs, common burdock	Anne Elliott www.flickr.com/photos/annkelliott
67	Prioritizing Grid	© Dick Bolles (What Color Is Your Parchute?) www.jobhuntersbible.com
94	Joke scramble	Michael Jursic
105	Dandelion (balloon hair)	Heidi Hoopes www.flickr.com/photos/meer/23396958/
110	Birthday party	Lance Cadena
115	Velcro opening slide	Tracy E. Anderson

Page	Description	Source/Info/Photograph by
124	Air race contrails	Nuno Gomez
125	Bouquets to Art	Margaret Lew www.pbase.com/mclew_flower_show
127	Data vs. pics	Lance Cadena
128	Velcro dog	Johny Day www.flickr.com/photos/johnydaystudio
137	Varkala beach	Rashmi Sinha
172	HeartMath "doughnut"	www.heartmath.org/research/research-home/research-center-home.html
174	Blair holding the sun	Blair by Wes Burmark. Sunset by Lynell Burmark. Photoshop composition by Lance Cadena.
195	Karly, rose	Wes Burmark
197	Penguin exhibit	Jerome Burg
198	Shanta	Rashmi Sinha
209	tangerines	Lance Cadena
211	Cut lemons	© Rob Tunstall www.flickr.com/photos/baldmonk
222	Leaves	www.scottliddell.net
222	Daffodil	Davehamilton1964@aol.com
223	Stacie stretch	Lance Cadena

How to use the DVD

System requirements

PC with Microsoft Windows 2003 or later

Mac with Apple OS version 10.1 or later

Using the DVD with Windows

To view the items located on the DVD, follow these steps:

1. Insert the DVD into your computer's DVD drive.

2. A window will open asking you to select "Run start.exe" or "Open folder to view files."

3. Double-click "Run start.exe" to launch the DVD

If you do not have autorun enabled, or if the autorun window does not appear, follow these steps to access the DVD:

1. Click Start → Run.

2. In the dialog box that appears, type d:\start.exe, where d is the letter of your DVD drive. This brings up the autorun window described in the preceding set of steps.

3. Choose the desired option from the menu. (See Step 2 in the preceding list for a description of these options.)

   Using the DVD With Apple OS

   Insert the DVD into the DVD drive. When the DVD is mounted, a window showing the DVD contents will automatically launch.

   Double-click the file named "Start". The DVD interface will open.

In case of trouble

If you experience difficulty using the DVD, please follow these steps:

1. Make sure your hardware and systems configurations conform to the systems requirements noted under "System Requirements" above.

2. Review the installation procedure for your type of hardware and operating system. It is possible to reinstall the software if necessary.

To speak with someone in Product Technical Support, call 800-762-2974 or 317-572-3994 Monday through Friday from 8:30 A.M. to 5:00 P.M. EST. You can also contact Product Technical Support and get support information through our website at www.wiley.com/techsupport.

Before calling or writing, please have the following information available:

- Type of computer and operating system.

- Any error messages displayed.

- Complete description of the problem.

It is best if you are sitting at your computer when making the call.